The World's Last Night

And Other Essays

BOOKS BY C. S. LEWIS

The Pilgrim's Regress
The Problem of Pain
The Screwtape Letters *and* Screwtape Proposes a Toast
Broadcast Talks
The Abolition of Man
Christian Behaviour
Beyond Personality
The Great Divorce
George MacDonald: An Anthology
Miracles
Transposition and Other Addresses
Mere Christianity
Surprised by Joy: The Shape of My Early Life
Reflections on the Psalms
The World's Last Night and Other Essays
The Four Loves
Letters to Malcolm: Chiefly on Prayer
Poems
Of Other Worlds: Essays and Stories
Letters of C. S. Lewis
Narrative Poems
A Mind Awake: An Anthology of C. S. Lewis
On Stories: And Other Essays on Literature
Spirits in Bondage: A Cycle of Lyrics
The Business of Heaven: Daily Readings from C. S. Lewis
Present Concerns
All My Road Before Me: The Diary of C. S. Lewis, 1922–1927

For Children
THE CHRONICLES OF NARNIA:
The Lion, the Witch and the Wardrobe
Prince Caspian
The Voyage of the *Dawn Treader*
The Silver Chair
The Horse and His Boy
The Magician's Nephew
The Last Battle

Fiction
Out of the Silent Planet
Perelandra
That Hideous Strength
Till We Have Faces: A Myth Retold
The Dark Tower and Other Stories
Boxen: The Imaginary World of the Young C. S. Lewis

C. S. LEWIS

The World's Last Night

And Other Essays

A HARVEST BOOK • HARCOURT, INC.
San Diego   New York   London

"The Efficacy of Prayer" appeared in the *Atlantic Monthly* (January, 1959);
"On Obstinacy in Belief," a paper read to the Socratic Club, Oxford,in the
Sewanee Review (Autumn, 1955); "Lilies That Fester" in the *Twentieth
Century* (April, 1955); "Screwtape Proposes a Toast" in the *Saturday Evening
Post* (December, 1959); "Good Work and Good Works" in *Catholic Art
Quarterly* (Christmas, 1959); "Religion and Rocketry" in *Christian Herald* (as
"Will We Lose God in Outer Space?") (April, 1958); "The World's Last Night"
in *Religion for Life* (as "The Christian Hope — Its Meaning for Today")
(Winter, 1952).

Library of Congress Cataloging-in-Publication Data
Lewis, Clive Staples, 1898–1963.
The world's last night.
(A Harvest book)
CONTENTS: The efficacy of prayer. — On obsintacy
in belief. — Lilies that fester. — Screwtape proposes
a toast. [etc.]
1. Christianity — Addresses, essays, lectures.
I. Title.
[BR123.L487   1973]   201'.1   73-4887
ISBN 0-15-602771-2

Printed in the United States of America

F H J I G E

CONTENTS

THE WORLD'S LAST NIGHT
AND OTHER ESSAYS

Some years ago I got up one morning intending to have my hair cut in preparation for a visit to London, and the first letter I opened made it clear I need not go to London. So I decided to put the haircut off too. But then there began the most unaccountable little nagging in my mind, almost like a voice saying, "Get it cut all the same. Go and get it cut." In the end I could stand it no longer. I went. Now my barber at that time was a fellow Christian and a man of many troubles whom my brother and I had sometimes been able to help. The moment I opened his shop door he said, "Oh, I was praying you might come today." And in fact if I had come a day or so later I should have been of no use to him.

It awed me; it awes me still. But of course one cannot rigorously prove a causal connection between the barber's prayers and my visit. It might be telepathy. It might be accident.

I have stood by the bedside of a woman whose thighbone was eaten through with cancer and who had thriving colonies of the disease in many other bones as well.

3

It took three people to move her in bed. The doctors predicted a few months of life; the nurses (who often know better), a few weeks. A good man laid his hands on her and prayed. A year later the patient was walking (uphill, too, through rough woodland) and the man who took the last X-ray photos was saying, "These bones are as solid as rock. It's miraculous."

But once again there is no rigorous proof. Medicine, as all true doctors admit, is not an exact science. We need not invoke the supernatural to explain the falsification of its prophecies. You need not, unless you choose, believe in a causal connection between the prayers and the recovery.

The question then arises, "What sort of evidence *would* prove the efficacy of prayer?" The thing we pray for may happen, but how can you ever know it was not going to happen anyway? Even if the thing were indisputably miraculous it would not follow that the miracle had occurred because of your prayers. The answer surely is that a compulsive empirical proof such as we have in the sciences can never be attained.

Some things are proved by the unbroken uniformity of our experiences. The law of gravitation is established by the fact that, in our experience, all bodies without exception obey it. Now even if all the things that people prayed for happened, which they do not, this would not prove what Christians mean by the efficacy of prayer. For prayer is request. The essence of request, as distinct from compulsion, is that it may or may not be granted. And if an infinitely wise Being listens to the requests of

4

finite and foolish creatures, of course He will sometimes grant and sometimes refuse them. Invariable "success" in prayer would not prove the Christian doctrine at all. It would prove something much more like magic—a power in certain human beings to control, or compel, the course of nature.

There are, no doubt, passages in the New Testament which may seem at first sight to promise an invariable granting of our prayers. But that cannot be what they really mean. For in the very heart of the story we meet a glaring instance to the contrary. In Gethsemane the holiest of all petitioners prayed three times that a certain cup might pass from Him. It did not. After that the idea that prayer is recommended to us as a sort of infallible gimmick may be dismissed.

Other things are proved not simply by experience but by those artificially contrived experiences which we call experiments. Could this be done about prayer? I will pass over the objection that no Christian could take part in such a project, because he has been forbidden it: "You must not try experiments on God, your Master." Forbidden or not, is the thing even possible?

I have seen it suggested that a team of people—the more the better—should agree to pray as hard as they knew how, over a period of six weeks, for all the patients in Hospital A and none of those in Hospital B. Then you would tot up the results and see if A had more cures and fewer deaths. And I suppose you would repeat the experiment at various times and places so as to eliminate the influence of irrelevant factors.

The trouble is that I do not see how any real prayer could go on under such conditions. "Words without thoughts never to heaven go," says the King in *Hamlet*. Simply to say prayers is not to pray; otherwise a team of properly trained parrots would serve as well as men for our experiment. You cannot pray for the recovery of the sick unless the end you have in view is their recovery. But you can have no motive for desiring the recovery of all the patients in one hospital and none of those in another. You are not doing it in order that suffering should be relieved; you are doing it to find out what happens. The real purpose and the nominal purpose of your prayers are at variance. In other words, whatever your tongue and teeth and knees may do, you are not praying. The experiment demands an impossibility.

Empirical proof and disproof are, then, unobtainable. But this conclusion will seem less depressing if we remember that prayer is request and compare it with other specimens of the same thing.

We make requests of our fellow creatures as well as of God: we ask for the salt, we ask for a raise in pay, we ask a friend to feed the cat while we are on our holidays, we ask a woman to marry us. Sometimes we get what we ask for and sometimes not. But when we do, it is not nearly so easy as one might suppose to prove with scientific certainty a causal connection between the asking and the getting.

Your neighbour may be a humane person who would not have let your cat starve even if you had forgotten to make any arrangement. Your employer is never so likely to grant your request for a raise as when he is aware that you could get better money from a rival firm and is quite possibly intending to secure you by a raise in any case. As for the lady who consents to marry you—are you sure she had not decided to do so already? Your proposal, you know, might have been the result, not the cause, of her decision. A certain important conversation might never have taken place unless she had intended that it should.

Thus in some measure the same doubt that hangs about the causal efficacy of our prayers to God hangs also about our prayers to man. Whatever we get we might have been going to get anyway. But only, as I say, in some measure. Our friend, boss, and wife may tell us that they acted because we asked; and we may know them so well as to feel sure, first that they are saying what they believe to be true, and secondly that they understand their own motives well enough to be right. But notice that when this happens our assurance has not been gained by the methods of science. We do not try the control experiment of refusing the raise or breaking off the engagement and then making our request again under fresh conditions. Our assurance is quite different in kind from scientific knowledge. It is born out of our personal relation to the other parties; not from knowing things about them but from knowing *them*.

Our assurance—if we reach an assurance—that God always hears and sometimes grants our prayers, and that apparent grantings are not merely fortuitous, can only come in the same sort of way. There can be no question of tabulating successes and failures and trying to decide whether the successes are too numerous to be accounted for by chance. Those who best know a man best know whether, when he did what they asked, he did it because they asked. I think those who best know God will best know whether He sent me to the barber's shop because the barber prayed.

For up till now we have been tackling the whole question in the wrong way and on the wrong level. The very question "Does prayer work?" puts us in the wrong frame of mind from the outset. "Work": as if it were magic, or a machine—something that functions automatically. Prayer is either a sheer illusion or a personal contact between embryonic, incomplete persons (ourselves) and the utterly concrete Person. Prayer in the sense of petition, asking for things, is a small part of it; confession and penitence are its threshold, adoration its sanctuary, the presence and vision and enjoyment of God its bread and wine. In it God shows Himself to us. That He answers prayers is a corollary—not necessarily the most important one—from that revelation. What He does is learned from what He is.

Petitionary prayer is, nonetheless, both allowed and commanded to us: "Give us our daily bread." And no doubt it raises a theoretical problem. Can we believe that God ever really modifies His action in response to the suggestions of men? For infinite wisdom does not need telling what is best, and infinite goodness needs no urging to do it. But neither does God need any of those things that are done by finite agents, whether

8

living or inanimate. He could, if He chose, repair our bodies miraculously without food; or give us food without the aid of farmers, bakers, and butchers; or knowledge without the aid of learned men; or convert the heathen without missionaries. Instead, He allows soils and weather and animals and the muscles, minds, and wills of men to co-operate in the execution of His will. "God," said Pascal, "instituted prayer in order to lend to His creatures the dignity of causality." But not only prayer; whenever we act at all He lends us that dignity. It is not really stranger, nor less strange, that my prayers should affect the course of events than that my other actions should do so. They have not advised or changed God's mind—that is, His over-all purpose. But that purpose will be realized in different ways according to the actions, including the prayers, of His creatures.

For He seems to do nothing of Himself which He can possibly delegate to His creatures. He commands us to do slowly and blunderingly what He could do perfectly and in the twinkling of an eye. He allows us to neglect what He would have us do, or to fail. Perhaps we do not fully realize the problem, so to call it, of enabling finite free wills to co-exist with Omnipotence. It seems to involve at every moment almost a sort of divine abdication. We are not mere recipients or spectators. We are either privileged to share in the game or compelled to collaborate in the work, "to wield our little tridents." Is this amazing process simply Creation going on before our eyes? This is how (no light matter) God makes something—indeed, makes gods—out of nothing.

So at least it seems to me. But what I have offered can be, at the very best, only a mental model or symbol. All that we say on such subjects must be merely analogical and parabolic. The reality is doubtless not comprehensible by our faculties. But we can at any rate try to expel bad analogies and bad parables. Prayer is not a machine. It is not magic. It is not advice offered to God. Our act, when we pray, must not, any more than all our other acts, be separated from the continuous act of God Himself, in which alone all finite causes operate.

It would be even worse to think of those who get what they pray for as a sort of court favorites, people who have influence with the throne. The refused prayer of Christ in Gethsemane is answer enough to that. And I dare not leave out the hard saying which I once heard from an experienced Christian: "I have seen many striking answers to prayer and more than one that I thought miraculous. But they usually come at the beginning: before conversion, or soon after it. As the Christian life proceeds, they tend to be rarer. The refusals, too, are not only more frequent; they become more unmistakable, more emphatic."

Does God then forsake just those who serve Him best? Well, He who served Him best of all said, near His tortured death, "Why hast thou forsaken me?" When God becomes man, that Man, of all others, is least comforted by God, at His greatest need. There is a mystery here which, even if I had the power, I might not have the courage to explore. Meanwhile, little people like you and me, if our prayers are sometimes granted, beyond all hope and probability, had better not draw hasty conclusions to our own advantage. If we were stronger, we might be less tenderly treated. If we were braver, we might be sent, with far less help, to defend far more desperate posts in the great battle.

Papers have more than once been read to the Socratic Club at Oxford in which a contrast was drawn between a supposedly Christian attitude and a supposedly scientific attitude to belief. We have been told that the scientist thinks it his duty to proportion the strength of his belief exactly to the evidence; to believe less as there is less evidence and to withdraw belief altogether when reliable adverse evidence turns up. We have been told that, on the contrary, the Christian regards it as positively praiseworthy to believe without evidence, or in excess of the evidence, or to maintain his belief unmodified in the teeth of steadily increasing evidence against it. Thus a "faith that has stood firm," which appears to mean a belief immune from all the assaults of reality, is commended.

If this were a fair statement of the case, then the coexistence within the same species of such scientists and such Christians would be a very staggering phenomenon. The fact that the two classes appear to overlap, as they do, would be quite inexplicable. Certainly all discussion between creatures so different would be hope-

13

less. The purpose of this essay is to show that things are really not quite so bad as that. The sense in which scientists proportion their belief to the evidence, and the sense in which Christians do not, both need to be defined more closely. My hope is that when this has been done, though disagreement between the two parties may remain, they will not be left staring at one another in wholly dumb and desperate incomprehension.

And first, a word about belief in general. I do not see that the state of "proportioning belief to evidence" is anything like so common in the scientific life as has been claimed. Scientists are mainly concerned not with believing things but with finding things out. And no one, to the best of my knowledge, uses the word "believe" about things he has found out. The doctor says he "believes" a man was poisoned before he has examined the body; after the examination, he says the man was poisoned. No one says that he believes the multiplication table. No one who catches a thief red-handed says he believes that man was stealing. The scientist, when at work, that is, when he is a scientist, is labouring to escape from belief and unbelief into knowledge. Of course he uses hypotheses or supposals. I do not think these are beliefs. We must look, then, for the scientist's behaviour about belief not to his scientific life but to his leisure hours.

In actual modern English usage the verb "believe," except for two special usages, generally expresses a very weak degree of opinion. "Where is Tom?" "Gone to London, I believe." The speaker would be only mildly surprised if Tom had not gone to London after all. "What was the date?" "430 B.C., I believe." The speaker means that he is far from sure. It is the same with the negative if it is put in the form "I believe not." ("Is Jones coming up this term?" "I believe not.") But if the negative is put in a different form it then becomes one of the special usages I mentioned a moment ago. This is of course the form "I don't believe it," or the still stronger "I don't believe you." "I don't believe it" is far stronger on the negative side than "I believe" is on the positive. "Where is Mrs. Jones?" "Eloped with the butler, I believe." "I don't believe it." This, especially if said with anger, may imply a conviction which in subjective certitude might be hard to distinguish from knowledge by experience. The other special usage is "I believe" as uttered by a Christian. There is no great difficulty in making the hardened materialist understand, however little he approves, the sort of mental attitude which this "I believe" expresses. The materialist need only picture himself replying, to some report of a miracle, "I don't believe it," and then imagine this same degree of conviction on the opposite side. He knows that he cannot, there and then, produce a refutation of the miracle which would have the certainty of mathematical demonstration; but the formal possibility that the miracle might after all have occurred does not really trouble him any more than a fear that water might not be H and O. Similarly, the Christian does not necessarily claim to have demonstrative proof; but the formal possibility that God might not exist is not necessarily present in the form of the least actual doubt. Of course there are Christians who hold that such demonstrative proof exists, just as there may be materialists who hold that there is demonstrative disproof. But then, whichever of them is right (if either is) while he retained the proof or disproof would be not believing or disbelieving but knowing. We are speaking of belief and disbelief in the strongest degree, but not of knowledge. Belief, in this sense, seems to me to be assent to a proposition which we think so overwhelmingly probable that there is a psychological exclusion of doubt, though not a logical exclusion of dispute.

It may be asked whether belief (and of course disbelief) of this sort ever attaches to any but theological propositions. I think that many beliefs approximate to it; that is, many probabilities seem to us so strong that the absence of logical certainty does not induce in us the least shade of doubt. The scientific beliefs of those who are not themselves scientists often have this character, especially among the uneducated. Most of our beliefs about other people are of the same sort. The scientist himself, or he who was a scientist in the laboratory, has beliefs about his wife and friends which he holds, not indeed without evidence, but with more certitude than the evidence, if weighed in the laboratory manner, would justify. Most of my generation had a belief in the reality of the external world and of other people—if you prefer it, a disbelief in solipsism—far in excess of our strongest arguments. It may be true, as they now say, that the whole thing arose from category mistakes and was a pseudo-problem; but then we didn't know that in the twenties. Yet we managed to disbelieve in solipsism all the same.

There is, of course, no question so far of belief without evidence. We must beware of confusion between the way in which a Christian first assents to certain propositions and the way in which he afterwards adheres to them. These must be carefully distinguished. Of the second it is true, in a sense, to say that Christians do recommend a certain discounting of apparent contrary evidence, and I will later attempt to explain why. But so far as I know it is not expected that a man should assent to these propositions in the first place without evidence or in the teeth of the evidence. At any rate, if anyone expects that, I certainly do not. And in fact, the man who accepts Christianity always thinks he had good evidence; whether, like Dante, *fisici e metafisici argomenti,* or historical evidence, or the evidence of religious experience, or authority, or all these together. For of course authority, however we may value it in this or that particular instance, is a kind of evidence. All of our historical beliefs, most of our geographical beliefs, many of our beliefs about matters that concern us in daily life, are accepted on the authority of other human beings, whether we are Christians, Atheists, Scientists, or Men-in-the-Street.

It is not the purpose of this essay to weigh the evidence, of whatever kind, on which Christians base their belief. To do that would be to write a full-dress *apologia.* All that I need do here is to point out that, at the very worst, this evidence cannot be so weak as to warrant the view that all whom it convinces are indifferent to evidence. The history of thought seems to make this quite plain. We know, in fact, that believers are not cut off from unbelievers by any portentous inferiority of intelligence or any perverse refusal to think. Many of them have been people of powerful minds. Many of them have been scientists. We may suppose them to have been mistaken, but we must suppose that their error was at least plausible. We might, indeed, conclude that it was, merely from the multitude and diversity of the arguments against it. For there is not one case against religion, but many. Some say, like Capaneus in Statius, that it is a projection of our primitive fears, *primus in orbe deos fecit timor:* others, with Euhemerus, that it is all a "plant" put up by wicked kings, priests, or capitalists; others, with Tylor, that it comes from dreams about the dead; others, with Frazer, that it is a by-product of agriculture; others, like Freud, that it is a complex; the moderns that it is a category mistake. I will never believe that an error against which so many and various defensive weapons have been found necessary was, from the outset, wholly lacking in plausibility. All this "post haste and rummage in the land" obviously implies a respectable enemy.

There are of course people in our own day to whom the whole situation seems altered by the doctrine of the concealed wish. They will admit that men, otherwise apparently rational, have been deceived by the arguments for religion. But they will say that they have been deceived first by their own desires and produced the arguments afterwards as a rationalization: that these arguments have never been intrinsically even plausible, but have seemed so because they were secretly weighted by our wishes. Now I do not doubt that this sort of thing happens in thinking about religion as in thinking about other things; but as a general explanation of religious assent it seems to me quite useless. On that issue our wishes may favour either side or both. The assumption that every man would be pleased, and nothing but pleased, if only he could conclude that Christianity is true, appears to me to be simply preposterous. If Freud is right about the Oedipus complex, the universal pressure of the wish that God should not exist must be enormous, and atheism must be an admirable gratification to one of our strongest suppressed impulses. This argument, in fact, could be used on the theistic side. But I have no intention of so using it. It will not really help either party. It is fatally ambivalent. Men wish on both sides: and again, there is fear-fulfilment as well as wish-fulfilment, and hypochondriac temperaments will always tend to think true what they most wish to be false. Thus instead of the one predicament on which our opponents sometimes concentrate there are in fact four. A man may be a Christian because he wants Christianity to be true. He may be an atheist because he wants atheism to be true. He may be an atheist because he wants Christianity to be true. He may be a Christian because he wants atheism to be true. Surely these possibilities cancel one another out? They may be

of some use in analysing a particular instance of belief
or disbelief, where we know the case history, but as a
general explanation of either they will not help us. I
do not think they overthrow the view that there is evidence both for and against the Christian propositions
which fully rational minds, working honestly, can assess
differently.

I therefore ask you to substitute a different and less
tidy picture for that with which we began. In it, you remember, two different kinds of men, scientists, who
proportioned their belief to the evidence, and Christians, who did not, were left facing one another across a
chasm The picture I should prefer is like this. All men
alike, on questions which interest them, escape from
the region of belief into that of knowledge when they
can, and if they succeed in knowing, they no longer say
they believe. The questions in which mathematicians
are interested admit of treatment by a particularly clear
and strict technique. Those of the scientist have their
own technique, which is not quite the same. Those of
the historian and the judge are different again. The
mathematician's proof (at least so we laymen suppose)
is by reasoning, the scientist's by experiment, the historian's by documents, the judge's by concurring sworn
testimony. But all these men, as men, on questions outside their own disciplines, have numerous beliefs to
which they do not normally apply the methods of their
own disciplines. It would indeed carry some suspicion
of morbidity and even of insanity if they did. These beliefs vary in strength from weak opinion to complete

subjective certitude. Specimens of such beliefs at their strongest are the Christian's "I believe" and the convinced atheist's "I don't believe a word of it." The particular subject-matter on which these two disagree does not, of course, necessarily involve such strength of belief and disbelief. There are some who moderately opine that there is, or is not, a God. But there are others whose belief or disbelief is free from doubt. And all these beliefs, weak or strong, are based on what appears to the holders to be evidence; but the strong believers or disbelievers of course think they have very strong evidence. There is no need to suppose stark unreason on either side. We need only suppose error. One side has estimated the evidence wrongly. And even so, the mistake cannot be supposed to be of a flagrant nature; otherwise the debate would not continue.

So much, then, for the way in which Christians come to assent to certain propositions. But we have now to consider something quite different; their adherence to their belief after it has once been formed. It is here that the charge of irrationality and resistance to evidence becomes really important. For it must be admitted at once that Christians do praise such an adherence as if it were meritorious; and even, in a sense, more meritorious the stronger the apparent evidence against their faith becomes. They even warn one another that such apparent contrary evidence—such "trials to faith" or "temptations to doubt"—may be expected to occur, and determine in advance to resist them. And this is certainly shockingly unlike the behaviour we all demand of the scientist or the historian in their own disciplines. There, to slur over or ignore the faintest evidence against a favourite hypothesis, is admittedly foolish and shameful. It must be exposed to every test; every doubt must be invited. But then I do not admit that a hypothesis is a belief. And if we consider the scientist not among his hypotheses in the laboratory but among the beliefs in his ordinary life, I think the contrast between him and the Christian would be weakened. If, for the first time, a doubt of his wife's fidelity crosses the scientist's mind, does he consider it his duty at once to entertain this doubt with complete impartiality, at once to evolve a series of experiments by which it can be tested, and to await the result with pure neutrality of mind? No doubt it may come to that in the end. There are unfaithful wives; there are experimental husbands. But is such a course what his brother scientists would recommend to him (all of them, I suppose, except one) as the first step he should take and the only one consistent with his honour as a scientist? Or would they, like us, blame him for a moral flaw rather than praise him for an intellectual virtue if he did so?

This is intended, however, merely as a precaution against exaggerating the difference between Christian obstinacy in belief and the behaviour of normal people about their non-theological beliefs. I am far from suggesting that the case I have supposed is exactly parallel to the Christian obstinacy. For of course evidence of the wife's infidelity might accumulate, and presently reach a point at which the scientist would be pitiably foolish to disbelieve it. But the Christians seem to praise an adherence to the original belief which holds out against any evidence whatever. I must now try to show why such praise is in fact a logical conclusion from the original belief itself.

This can be done best by thinking for a moment of situations in which the thing is reversed. In Christianity such faith is demanded of us; but there are situations in which we demand it of others. There are times when we can do all that a fellow creature needs if only he will trust us. In getting a dog out of a trap, in extracting a thorn from a child's finger, in teaching a boy to swim or rescuing one who can't, in getting a frightened beginner over a nasty place on a mountain, the one fatal obstacle may be their distrust. We are asking them to trust us in the teeth of their senses, their imagination, and their intelligence. We ask them to believe that what is painful will relieve their pain and that what looks dangerous is their only safety. We ask them to accept apparent impossibilities: that moving the paw farther back into the trap is the way to get it out—that hurting the finger very much more will stop the finger hurting —that water which is obviously permeable will resist and support the body—that holding onto the only support within reach is not the way to avoid sinking—that to go higher and onto a more exposed ledge is the way not to fall. To support all these *incredibilia* we can rely only on the other party's confidence in us—a confidence certainly not based on demonstration, admittedly shot through with emotion, and perhaps, if we are strangers, resting on nothing but such assurance as the look of our face and the tone of our voice can supply, or even, for the dog, on our smell. Sometimes, because of their unbelief, we can do no mighty works. But if we succeed, we do so because they have maintained their faith in us against apparently contrary evidence. No one blames us for demanding such faith. No one blames them for giving it. No one says afterwards what an unintelligent dog or child or boy that must have been to trust us. If the young mountaineer were a scientist, it would not be held against him, when he came up for a fellowship, that he had once departed from Clifford's rule of evidence by entertaining a belief with strength greater than the evidence logically obliged him to.

Now to accept the Christian propositions is *ipso facto* to believe that we are to God, always, as that dog or child or bather or mountain climber was to us, only very much more so. From this it is a strictly logical conclusion that the behaviour which was appropriate to them will be appropriate to us, only very much more so. Mark: I am not saying that the strength of our original belief must by psychological necessity produce such behaviour. I am saying that the content of our original belief by logical necessity entails the proposition that such behaviour is appropriate. If human life is in fact ordered by a beneficent being whose knowledge of our real needs and of the way in which they can be satisfied infinitely exceeds our own, we must expect *a priori* that His operations will often appear to us far from beneficent and far from wise, and that it will be our highest prudence to give Him our confidence in spite of this. This expectation is increased by the fact that when we accept Christianity we are warned that apparent evidence against it will occur—evidence strong enough "to deceive if possible the very elect." Our situation is rendered tolerable by two facts. One is that we seem to ourselves, besides the apparently contrary evidence, to receive favourable evidence. Some of it is in the form of external events: as when I go to see a man, moved by what I felt to be a whim, and find he has been praying that I should come to him that day. Some of it is more like the evidence on which the mountaineer or the dog might trust his rescuer—the rescuer's voice, look, and smell. For it seems to us (though you, on your premises, must believe us deluded) that we have something like a knowledge-by-acquaintance of the Person we believe in, however imperfect and intermittent it may be. We trust not because "a God" exists, but because *this* God exists. Or if we ourselves dare not claim to "know" Him, Christendom does, and we trust at least some of its representatives in the same way: because of the sort of people they are. The second fact is this. We think we can see already why, if our original belief is true, such trust beyond the evidence, against much apparent evidence, has to be demanded of us. For the question is not about being helped out of one trap or over one difficult place in a climb. We believe that His intention is to create a certain personal relation between Himself and us, a relation really *sui generis* but analogically describable in terms of filial or of erotic love. Complete trust is an ingredient in that relation—such trust as could have no room to grow except where there is also room for doubt. To love involves trusting the beloved beyond the evidence, even against much evidence. No man is our friend who believes in our good intentions only when they are proved. No man is our friend who will not be very slow to accept evidence against them. Such confidence, between one man and another, is in fact almost universally praised as a moral beauty, not blamed as a logical error. And the suspicious man is blamed for a meanness of character, not admired for the excellence of his logic.

There is, you see, no real parallel between Christian obstinacy in faith and the obstinacy of a bad scientist trying to preserve a hypothesis although the evidence has turned against it. Unbelievers very pardonably get the impression that an adherence to our faith is like that, because they meet Christianity, if at all, mainly in apologetic works. And there, of course, the existence and beneficence of God must appear as a speculative question like any other. Indeed, it is a speculative question as long as it is a question at all. But once it has been answered in the affirmative, you get quite a new situation. To believe that God—at least *this* God—exists is to believe that you as a person now stand in the presence of God as a Person. What would, a moment before, have been variations in opinion, now become variations in your personal attitude to a Person. You are no longer faced with an argument which demands your assent, but with a Person who demands your confidence. A faint analogy would be this. It is one thing to ask *in vacuo* whether So-and-So will join us tonight, and another to discuss this when So-and-So's honour is pledged to come and some great matter depends on his coming. In the first case it would be merely reasonable, as the clock ticked on, to expect him less and less. In the second, a continued expectation far into the night would be due to our friend's character if we had found him reliable before. Which of us would not feel slightly ashamed if, one moment after we had given him up, he arrived with a full explanation of his delay? We should feel that we ought to have known him better.

Now of course we see, quite as clearly as you, how agonizingly two-edged all this is. A faith of this sort, if it happens to be true, is obviously what we need, and it is infinitely ruinous to lack it. But there can be faith of this sort where it is wholly ungrounded. The dog may lick the face of the man who comes to take it out of the trap; but the man may only mean to vivisect it in South Parks Road when he has done so. The ducks who come to the call "Dilly, dilly, come and be killed" have confidence in the farmer's wife, and she wrings their necks for their pains. There is that famous French story of the fire in the theatre. Panic was spreading, the spectators were just turning from an audience into a mob. At that moment a huge bearded man leaped through the orchestra onto the stage, raised his hand with a gesture full of nobility, and cried, *"Que chacun regagne sa place."* Such was the authority of his voice and bearing that everyone obeyed him. As a result they were all burned to death, while the bearded man walked quietly out through the wings to the stage door, took a cab which was waiting for someone else, and went home to bed.

That demand for our confidence which a true friend makes of us is exactly the same that a confidence trickster would make. That refusal to trust, which is sensible in reply to a confidence trickster, is ungenerous and ignoble to a friend, and deeply damaging to our relation with him. To be forewarned and therefore forearmed against apparently contrary appearance is eminently rational if our belief is true; but if our belief is a delusion, this same forewarning and forearming would obviously be the method whereby the delusion rendered itself incurable. And yet again, to be aware of these possibilities and still to reject them is clearly the precise mode, and the only mode, in which our personal response to God can establish itself. In that sense the ambiguity is not something that conflicts with faith so much as a condition which makes faith possible. When you are asked for trust you may give it or withhold it; it is senseless to say that you will trust if you are given demonstrative certainty. There would be no room for trust if demonstration were given. When demonstration is given what will be left will be simply the sort of relation which results from having trusted, or not having trusted, before it was given.

The saying "Blessed are those that have not seen and have believed" has nothing to do with our original assent to the Christian propositions. It was not addressed to a philosopher enquiring whether God exists. It was addressed to a man who already believed that, who already had long acquaintance with a particular Person, and evidence that that Person could do very odd things, and who then refused to believe one odd thing more, often predicted by that Person and vouched for by all his closest friends. It is a rebuke not to scepticism in the philosophic sense but to the psychological quality of being "suspicious." It says in effect, "You should have known me better." There are cases between man and man where we should all, in our different way, bless those who have not seen and have believed. Our relation to those who trusted us only after we were proved innocent in court cannot be the same as our relation to those who trusted us all through.

Our opponents, then, have a perfect right to dispute with us about the grounds of our original assent. But they must not accuse us of sheer insanity if, after the assent has been given, our adherence to it is no longer proportioned to every fluctuation of the apparent evidence. They cannot of course be expected to know on what our assurance feeds, and how it revives and is always rising from its ashes. They cannot be expected to see how the *quality* of the object which we think we are beginning to know by acquaintance drives us to the view that if this were a delusion then we should have to say that the universe had produced no real thing of comparable value and that all explanations of the delusion seemed somehow less important than the thing explained. That is knowledge we cannot communicate. But they can see how the assent, of necessity, moves us from the logic of speculative thought into what might perhaps be called the logic of personal relations. What would, up till then, have been variations simply of opinion become variations of conduct by a person to a Person. *Credere Deum esse* turns into *Credere in Deum.* And *Deum* here is this God, the increasingly knowable Lord.

I<small>N</small> THE "Cambridge Number" of the *Twentieth Century* (1955) Mr. John Allen asked why so many people "go to such lengths to prove to us that really they are not intellectuals at all and certainly not cultured." I believe I know the answer. Two parallels may help to ease it into the reader's mind.

We all know those who shudder at the word *refinement* as a term of social approval. Sometimes they express their dislike of this usage by facetiously spelling it *refanement,* with the implication that it is likely to be commonest in the mouths of those whose speech has a certain varnished vulgarity. And I suppose we can all understand the shudder, whether we approve it or not. He who shudders feels that the quality of mind and behaviour which we call *refined* is nowhere less likely to occur than among those who aim at, and talk much about, *refinement.* Those who have this quality are not obeying any idea of *refinement* when they abstain from swaggering, spitting, snatching, triumphing, calling names, boasting or contradicting. These modes of behaviour do not occur to them as possibles: if they did, that training and sensibility which constitute refinement would reject them as disagreeables without reference to any ideal of conduct, just as we reject a bad egg without reference to its possible effect on our stomachs. *Refinement,* in fact, is a name given to certain behaviour from without. From within, it does not appear as *refinement;* indeed, it does not appear, does not become an object of consciousness, at all. Where it is most named it is most absent.

I produce my next parallel with many different kinds of reluctance. But I think it too illuminating to be omitted. The word *religion* is extremely rare in the New Testament or the writings of mystics. The reason is simple. Those attitudes and practises to which we give the collective name of *religion* are themselves concerned with religion hardly at all. To be religious is to have one's attention fixed on God and on one's neighbour in relation to God. Therefore, almost by definition, a religious man, or a man when he is being religious, is not thinking about *religion;* he hasn't the time. *Religion* is what we (or he himself at a later moment) call his activity from outside.

Of course those who disdain the words *refinement* and *religion* may be doing so from bad motives; they may wish to impress us with the idea that they are well-bred or holy. Such people are regarding chatter about *refinement* or *religion* simply as symptomatic of vulgarity or worldliness, and eschew the symptom to clear themselves from the suspicion of the disease. But there are others who sincerely and (I believe) rightly think that such talk is not merely a symptom of, but a cause active in producing, that disease. The talk is inimical to the thing talked of, likely to spoil it where it exists and to prevent its birth where it is unborn.

Now *culture* seems to belong to the same class of dangerous and embarrassing words. Whatever else it may mean, it certainly covers deep and genuine enjoyment of literature and the other arts. (By using the word *enjoyment* I do not mean to beg the vexed question about the rôle of pleasure in our experience of the arts. I mean *frui,* not *delectari;* as we speak of a man "enjoying" good health or an estate.) Now if I am certain of anything in the world, I am certain that while a man is, in this sense, enjoying *Don Giovanni* or the *Oresteia* he is not caring one farthing about *culture.* Culture? the irrelevance of it! For just as to be fat or clever means to be fatter or cleverer than most, so to be *cultured* must mean to be more so than most, and thus the very word carries the mind at once to comparisons, and groupings, and life in society. And what has all that to do with the horns that blow as the statue enters, or Clytæmnestra crying, "Now you have named me aright"? In *Howard's End* Mr. E. M. Forster excellently describes a girl listening to a symphony. She is not thinking about *culture:* nor about "Music"; nor even about "this music." She sees the whole world through the music. *Culture,* like religion, is a name given from outside to activities which are not themselves interested in *culture* at all, and would be ruined the moment they were.

I do not mean that we are never to talk of things from the outside. But when the things are of high value and very easily destroyed, we must talk with great care, and perhaps the less we talk the better. To be constantly engaged with the idea of *culture,* and (above all) of *culture* as something enviable, or meritorious, or something that confers prestige, seems to me to endanger those very "enjoyments" for whose sake we chiefly value it. If we encourage others, or ourselves, to hear, see, or read great art on the ground that it is a *cultured* thing to do, we call into play precisely those elements in us which must be in abeyance before we can enjoy art at all. We are calling up the desire for self-improvement, the desire for distinction, the desire to revolt (from one group) and to agree (with another), and a dozen busy passions which, whether good or bad in themselves, are, in relation to the arts, simply a blinding and paralysing distraction.

At this point some may protest that by *culture* they do not mean the "enjoyments" themselves, but the whole habit of mind which such experiences, re-acting upon one another, and reflected on, build up as a permanent possession. And some will wish to include the sensitive and enriching social life which, they think, will arise among groups of people who share this habit of mind. But this reinterpretation leaves me with the same difficulty. I can well imagine a lifetime of such enjoyments leading a man to such a habit of mind, but on one condition; namely, that he went to the arts for no such purpose. Those who read poetry to improve their minds will never improve their minds by reading poetry. For the true enjoyments must be spontaneous and compulsive and look to no remoter end. The Muses will submit to no marriage of convenience. The desirable habit of mind, if it is to come at all, must come as a by-product, unsought. The idea of making it one's aim suggests that shattering confidence which Goethe made to Eckermann: "In all my youthful amours the object I had in view was my own ennoblement." To this, I presume, most of us would reply that, even if we believe a love-affair can ennoble a young man, we feel sure that a love-affair undertaken for that purpose would fail of its object. Because of course it wouldn't be a love-affair at all.

So much for the individual. But the claims made for the "cultured" group raise an embarrassing question. What, exactly, is the evidence that *culture* produces among those who share it a sensitive and enriching social life? If by "sensitive" we mean "sensitive to real or imagined affronts," a case could be made out. Horace noted long ago that "bards are a touchy lot." The lives and writings of the Renaissance Humanists and the correspondence in the most esteemed literary periodicals of our own century will show that critics and scholars are the same. But *sensitive* in that meaning cannot be combined with *enriching*. Competitive and resentful egoisms can only impoverish social life. The sensitivity that enriches must be of the sort that guards a man from wounding others, not of the sort that makes him ready to feel wounded himself. Between this sensitivity and *culture*, my own experience does not suggest any causal connection. I have often found it among the uncultured. Among the cultured I have sometimes found it and sometimes not.

Let us be honest. I claim to be one of the cultured myself and have no wish to foul my own nest. Even if that claim is disallowed, I have at least lived among them and would not denigrate my friends. But we are speaking here among ourselves—behind closed doors. Frankness is best. The real traitor to our order is not the man who speaks, within that order, of its faults, but the man who flatters our corporate self-complacency. I gladly admit that we number among us men and women whose modesty, courtesy, fair-mindedness, patience in disputation and readiness to see an antagonist's point of view, are wholly admirable. I am fortunate to have known them. But we must also admit that we show as high a percentage as any group whatever of bullies, paranoiacs, and poltroons, of backbiters, exhibitionists, mopes, milksops, and world-without-end bores. The loutishness that turns every argument into a quarrel is really no rarer among us than among the sub-literate; the restless inferiority-complex ("stern to inflict" but not "stubborn to endure") which bleeds at a touch but scratches like a wildcat is almost as common among us as among schoolgirls.

If you doubt this, try an experiment. Take any one

of those who vaunt most highly the adjusting, cleansing, liberating, and civilising effects of *culture* and ask him about other poets, other critics, other scholars, not in the mass but one by one and name by name. Nine times out of ten he will deny of each what he claimed for all. He will certainly produce very few cases in which, on his own showing, *culture* has had its boasted results. Sometimes we suspect that he can think of only one. The conclusion most naturally to be drawn from his remarks is that the praise our order can most securely claim is that which Dr. Johnson gave to the Irish. "They are an honest people; they never speak well of one another."

It is then (at best) extremely doubtful whether *culture* produces any of those qualities which will enable people to associate with one another graciously, loyally, understandingly, and with permanent delight. When Ovid said that it "softened our manners," he was flattering a barbarian king. But even if *culture* did all these things, we could not embrace it for their sake. This would be to use consciously and self-consciously, as means to extraneous ends, things which must lose all their power of conducing to those ends by the very fact of being so used. For many modern exponents of *culture* seem to me to be "impudent" in the etymological sense; they lack *pudor*, they have no shyness where men ought to be shy. They handle the most precious and fragile things with the roughness of an auctioneer and talk of our most intensely solitary and fugitive experiences as if they were selling us a Hoover. It is all really very well summed up in Mr. Allen's phrase in the *Twentieth Century* "the faith in culture." A "faith in culture" is as bad as a faith in religion; both expressions imply a turning away from those very things which culture and religion are about. "Culture" as a collective name for certain very valuable activities is a permissible word; but *culture* hypostatized, set up on its own, made into a faith, a cause, a banner, a "platform," is unendurable. For none of the activities in question cares a straw for that faith or cause. It is like a return to early Semitic religion where names themselves were regarded as powers.

Now a step further. Mr. Allen complained that, not content with creeping out of earshot when we can bear the voices of certain *culture*-mongers no longer, we then wantonly consort, or pretend that we consort, with the lowest of the low-brows, and affect to share their pleasures. There are at this point (still p. 127) a good many allusions which go over my head. I don't know what A F N is, I am not fond of cellars, and modern whisky suits neither my purse, my palate, nor my digestion. But I think I know the sort of thing he has in mind, and I think I can account for it. As before, I will begin with a parallel. Suppose you had spent an evening among very young and very transparent snobs who were feigning a discriminating enjoyment of a great port, though anyone who knew could see very well that, if they had ever drunk port in their lives before, it came from a grocer's. And then suppose that on your journey home you went into a grubby little tea-shop and there heard an old body in a feather boa say to another old body, with a smack of her lips, "That was a nice cup o' tea, dearie, that was. Did me good." Would you not, at that moment, feel that this was like fresh mountain air? For here, at last, would be something real. Here would be a mind really concerned about that in which it expressed concern. Here would be pleasure, here would be un-debauched experience, spontaneous and compulsive, from the fountain-head. A live dog is better than a dead lion. In the same way, after a certain kind of sherry party, where there have been cataracts of *culture* but never one word or one glance that suggested a real enjoyment of any art, any person, or any natural object, my heart warms to the schoolboy on the bus who is reading *Fantasy and Science Fiction*, rapt and oblivious of all the world beside. For here also I should feel that I had met something real and live and unfabricated; genuine literary experience, spontaneous and compulsive, disinterested. I should have hopes of that boy. Those who have greatly cared for any book whatever may possibly come to care, some day, for good books. The organs of appreciation exist in them. They are not impotent. And even if this particular boy is never going to like anything severer than science-fiction, even so,

> *The child whose love is here, at least doth reap*
> *One precious gain, that he forgets himself.*

I should still prefer the live dog to the dead lion; perhaps, even, the wild dog to the over-tame poodle or Peke.

I should not have spent so many words on answering Mr. Allen's question (neither of us matters sufficiently to justify it) unless I thought that the discussion led to something of more consequence. This I will now try to develop. Mr. Forster feels anxious because he dreads Theocracy. Now if he expects to see a Theocracy set up in modern England, I myself believe his expectation to be wholly chimerical. But I wish to make it very clear that, if I thought the thing in the least probable, I should feel about it exactly as he does. I fully embrace the maxim (which he borrows from a Christian) that "all power corrupts." I would go further. The loftier the pretensions of the power, the more meddlesome, inhuman, and oppressive it will be. Theocracy is the worst of all possible governments. All political power is at best a necessary evil: but it is least evil when its sanctions are most modest and commonplace, when it claims no more than to be useful or convenient and sets itself strictly limited objectives. Anything transcendental or spiritual, or even anything very strongly ethical, in its pretensions is dangerous and encourages it to meddle with our private lives. Let the shoemaker stick to his last. Thus the Renaissance doctrine of Divine Right is for me a corruption of monarchy; Rousseau's General Will, of democracy; racial mysticisms, of nationality. And Theocracy, I admit and even insist, is the worst corruption of all. But then I don't think we are in any danger of it. What I think we are really in danger of is something that would be only one degree less intolerable, and intolerable in almost the same way.

I would call it Charientocracy; not the rule of the saints but the rule of the χαρίεντες, the *venustiores,* the Hotel de Rambouillet, the Wits, the Polite, the "Souls," the "Apostles," the Sensitive, the *Cultured,* the Integrated, or whatever the latest password may be. I will explain how I think it could come about.

The old social classes have broken up. Two results follow. On the one hand, since most men, as Aristotle observed, do not like to be merely equal with all other men, we find all sorts of people building themselves into groups within which they can feel superior to the mass; little unofficial, self-appointed aristocracies. The *Cultured* increasingly form such a group. Notice their tendency to use the social term *vulgar* of those who disagree with them. Notice that Mr. Allen spoke of rebels against, or deserters from, this group, as denying not that they are "intellectual" but that they are "intellectuals," not hiding a quality but deprecating inclusion in a class. On the other hand, inevitably, there is coming into existence a new, real, ruling class: what has been called the Managerial Class. The coalescence of these two groups, the unofficial, self-appointed aristocracy of the *Cultured* and the actual Managerial rulers, will bring us to Charientocracy.

But the two groups are already coalescing, because education is increasingly the means of access to the Managerial Class. And of course education, in some sense, is a very proper means of access; we do not want our rulers to be dunces. But education is coming to have a new significance. It aspires to do, and can do, far more to the pupil than education (except, perhaps, that of the Jesuits) has ever done before.

For one thing, the pupil is now far more defenceless in the hands of his teachers. He comes increasingly from businessmen's flats or workmen's cottages in which there are few books or none. He has hardly ever been alone. The educational machine seizes him very early and organizes his whole life, to the exclusion of all unsuperintended solitude or leisure. The hours of unsponsored, uninspected, perhaps even forbidden, reading, the ramblings, and the "long, long thoughts" in which those of luckier generations first discovered literature and nature and themselves are a thing of the past. If a Traherne or a Wordsworth were born to-day he would be "cured" before he was twelve. In short, the modern pupil is the ideal patient for those masters who, not content with teaching a subject, would create a character; helpless Plasticine. Or if by chance (for nature will be nature) he should have any powers of resistance, they know how to deal with him. I am coming to that point in a moment.

Secondly, the nature of the teaching has changed. In a sense it has changed for the better: that is, it demands far more of the master and, in recompense, makes his work more interesting. It has become far more intimate and penetrating; more inward. Not content with making sure that the pupil has read and remembered the text, it aspires to teach him appreciation. It seems harsh to quarrel with what at first sounds so reasonable an aim. Yet there is a danger in it. Everyone now laughs at the old test-paper with its context questions and the like, and people ask, "What good can that sort of thing do a boy?" But surely to demand that the test-paper should do the boy good is like demanding that a thermometer should heat a room. It was the reading of the text which was supposed to do the boy good; you set the paper to find out if he had read it. And just because the paper did not force the boy to produce, or to feign, appreciation, it left him free to develop in private, spontaneously, as an out-of-school activity which would never earn any marks, such appreciation as he could. That was a private affair between himself and Virgil or himself and Shakespeare. Nine times out of ten, probably, nothing happened at all. But whenever appreciation did occur (and quite certainly it sometimes did) it was genuine; suited to the boy's age and character; no exotic, but the healthy growth of its native soil and weather. But when we substitute exercises in "practical criticism" for the old, dry papers, a new situation arises. The boy will not get good marks (which means, in the long run, that he will not get into the Managerial Class) unless he produces the kind of responses, and the kind of analytic method, which commend themselves to his teacher. This means at best that he is trained to the precocious anticipation of responses, and of a method, inappropriate to his years. At worst it means that he is trained in the (not very difficult) art of simulating the orthodox responses. For nearly all boys are good mimics. Depend upon it, before you have been teaching for a term, everyone in the form knows pretty well "the sort of stuff that goes down with Prickly Pop-eye." In the crude old days they knew that what "went down," and the only thing that "went down" was correct answers to factual questions, and there were only two ways of producing those: working or cheating.

The thing would not be so bad if the responses which the pupils had to make were even those of the individual master. But we have already passed that stage. Somewhere (I have not yet tracked it down) there must be a kind of *culture*-mongers' central bureau which keeps a sharp look-out for deviationists. At least there is certainly someone who sends little leaflets to schoolmasters, printing half a dozen poems on each and telling the master not only which the pupils must be made to prefer, but exactly on what grounds. (The impertinence of it! We know what Mulcaster or Boyer would have done with those leaflets.)

Thus to say that, under the nascent régime, education alone will get you into the ruling class, may not mean simply that the failure to acquire certain knowledge and to reach a certain level of intellectual competence will exclude you. That would be reasonable enough. But it may come to mean, perhaps means already, something more. It means that you cannot get in without becoming, or without making your masters believe that you have become, a very specific kind of person, one who makes the right responses to the right authors. In fact, you can get in only by becoming, in the modern sense of the word, *cultured*. This situation must be distinguished from one that has often occurred be-

44

fore. Nearly all ruling classes, sooner or later, in some degree or other, have taken up *culture* and patronized the arts. But when that happens the *culture* is the result of their position; one of the luxuries or privileges of their order. The situation we are now facing will be almost the opposite. Entry into the ruling class will be the reward of *culture*. Thus we reach Charientocracy.

Not only is the thing likely to happen; it is already planned and avowed. Mr. J. W. Saunders has set it all out in an excellent article entitled "Poetry in the Managerial Age" (*Essays in Criticism,* iv, 3, July 1954). He there faces the fact that modern poets are read almost exclusively by one another. He looks about for a remedy. Naturally he does not suggest that the poets should do anything about it. For it is taken as basic by all the *culture* of our age that whenever artists and audience lose touch, the fault must be wholly on the side of the audience. (I have never come across the great work in which this important doctrine is proved.) The remedy which occurs to Mr. Saunders is that we should provide our poets with a conscript audience; a privilege last enjoyed, I believe, by Nero. And he tells us how this can be done. We get our "co-ordinators" through education; success in examinations is the road into the ruling class. All that we need do, therefore, is to make not just poetry, but "the intellectual discipline which the critical reading of poetry can foster," the backbone of our educational system. In other words, practical criticism or something of the sort, exercised, no doubt, chiefly on modern poets, is to be the indispensable subject, failure in which excludes you from the Managerial Class. And so our poets get their conscript readers. Every boy or girl who is born is presented with the choice: "Read the poets whom we, the *cultured,* approve, and say the sort of things we say about them, or be a prole." And this (picking up a previous point) shows how Charientocracy can deal with the minority of pupils who have tastes of their own and are not pure Plasticine. They get low marks. You kick them off the educational ladder at a low rung and they disappear into the proletariat.

Another advantage is that, besides providing poets with a conscript audience for the moment, you can make sure that the regnant literary dynasty will reign almost forever. For the deviationists whom you have kicked off the ladder will of course include all those troublesome types who, in earlier ages, were apt to start new schools and movements. If there had been a sound Charientocracy in their day, the young Chaucer, the young Donne, the young Wordsworth and Coleridge, could have been dealt with. And thus literary history, as we have known it in the past, may come to an end. Literary man, so long a wild animal, will have become a tame one.

Having explained why I think a Charientocracy probable, I must conclude by explaining why I think it undesirable.

Culture is a bad qualification for a ruling class because it does not qualify men to rule. The things we really need in our rulers—mercy, financial integrity, practical intelligence, hard work, and the like—are no more likely to be found in cultured persons than in anyone else.

Culture is a bad qualification in the same way as sanctity. Both are hard to diagnose and easy to feign. Of course not every charientocrat will be a cultural hypocrite nor every theocrat a Tartuffe. But both systems encourage hypocrisy and make the disinterested pursuit of the quality they profess to value more difficult.

But hypocrisy is not the only evil they encourage. There are, as in piety, so in *culture,* states which, if less culpable, are no less disastrous. In the one we have the "Goody-goody"; the docile youth who has neither revolted against nor risen above the routine pietisms and respectabilities of his home. His conformity has won the approval of his parents, his influential neighbours, and his own conscience. He does not know that he has missed anything and is content. In the other, we have the adaptable youth to whom poetry has always been something "Set" for "evaluation." Success in this exercise has given him pleasure and let him into the ruling class. He does not know what he has missed, does not know that poetry ever had any other purpose, and is content.

Both types are much to be pitied: but both can sometimes be very nasty. Both may exhibit spiritual pride, but each in its proper form, since the one has succeeded by acquiescence and repression, but the other by repeated victory in competitive performances. To the pride of the one, sly, simpering, and demure, we might apply Mr. Allen's word "smug" (especially if we let in a little of its older sense). My epithet for the other would, I think, be "swaggering." It tends in my experience to be raw, truculent, eager to give pain, insatiable in its demands for submission, resentful and suspicious of disagreement. Where the goody-goody slinks and sidles and purrs (and sometimes scratches) like a cat, his opposite number in the ranks of the *cultured* gobbles like an enraged turkey. And perhaps both types are less curable than the hypocrite proper. A hypocrite might (conceivably) repent and mend; or he might be unmasked and rendered innocuous. But who could bring to repentence, and who can unmask, those who were attempting no deception? who don't know that they are not the real thing because they don't know that there ever was a real thing?

Lastly I reach the point where my objections to Theocracy and to Charientocracy are almost identical. "Lilies that fester smell far worse than weeds." The higher the pretensions of our rulers are, the more meddlesome and impertinent their rule is likely to be and the more the thing in whose name they rule will be defiled. The highest things have the most precarious foothold in our nature. By making sanctity or culture a *moyen de parvenir* you help to drive them out of the world. Let our masters leave these two, at least, alone; leave us some region where the spontaneous, the unmarketable, the utterly private, can still exist.

As far as I am concerned, Mr. Allen fell short of the mark when he spoke of a "retreat from the faith in culture." I don't want retreat; I want attack or, if you prefer the word, rebellion. I write in the hope of rousing others to rebel. So far as I can see, the question has nothing to do with the difference between Christians and those who (unfortunately, since the word has long borne a useful, and wholly different, meaning) have been called "humanists." I hope that red herring will not be brought in. I would gladly believe that many atheists and agnostics care for the things I care for. It is for them I have written. To them I say: the "faith in culture" is going to strangle all those things unless we can strangle it first. And there is no time to spare.

FOUR
SCREWTAPE PROPOSES A TOAST

(The scene is in Hell at the annual dinner of the Tempters' Training College for young Devils. The Principal, Dr. Slubgob, has just proposed the health of the guests. Screwtape, a very experienced Devil, who is the guest of honour, rises to reply:)

Mr. PRINCIPAL, your Imminence, your Disgraces, my Thorns, Shadies, and Gentledevils:

It is customary on these occasions for the speaker to address himself chiefly to those among you who have just graduated and who will very soon be posted to official Temperships on Earth. It is a custom I willingly obey. I will remember with what trepidation I awaited my own first appointment. I hope, and believe, that each one of you has the same uneasiness tonight. Your career is before you. Hell expects and demands that it should be—as Mine was—one of unbroken success. If it is not, you know what awaits you.

I have no wish to reduce the wholesome and realistic element of terror, the unremitting anxiety, which must act as the lash and spur to your endeavors. How often you will envy the humans their faculty of sleep! Yet at the same time I would wish to put before you a moderately encouraging view of the strategical situation as a whole.

Your dreaded Principal has included in a speech full of points something like an apology for the banquet which he has set before us. Well, gentledevils, no one blames *him*. But it would be vain to deny that the human souls on whose anguish we have been feasting tonight were of pretty poor quality. Not all the most skilful cookery of our tormentors could make them better than insipid.

Oh to get one's teeth again into a Farinata, a Henry VIII, or even a Hitler! There was real crackling there; something to crunch; a rage, an egotism, a cruelty only just less robust than our own. It put up a delicious resistance to being devoured. It warmed your inwards when you'd got it down.

Instead of this, what have we had tonight? There was a municipal authority with Graft sauce. But personally I could not detect in him the flavour of a really passionate and brutal avarice such as delighted one in the great tycoons of the last century. Was he not unmistakably a Little Man—a creature of the petty rake-off pocketed with a petty joke in private and denied with the stalest platitudes in his public utterances—a grubby little nonentity who had drifted into corruption, only just realizing that he was corrupt, and chiefly because everyone else did it? Then there was the lukewarm Casserole of Adulterers. Could you find it in any trace of a fully inflamed, defiant, rebellious, insatiable lust? I couldn't. They all tasted to me like undersexed morons who had blundered or trickled into the wrong beds in automatic response to sexy advertisements, or to make themselves feel modern and emancipated, or to reassure themselves about their virility or their "normalcy," or even because they had nothing else to do. Frankly, to me who have tasted Messalina and Casanova, they were nauseating. The Trade Unionist stuffed with sedition was perhaps a shade better. He had done some real harm. He had, not quite unknowingly, worked for bloodshed, famine, and the extinction of liberty. Yes, in a way. But what a way! He thought of those ultimate objectives so little. Toeing the party line, self-importance, and above all mere routine, were what really dominated his life.

But now comes the point. Gastronomically, all this is deplorable. But I hope none of us puts gastronomy first. Is it not, in another and far more serious way, full of hope and promise?

Consider, first, the mere quantity. The quality may be wretched; but we never had souls (of a sort) in more abundance.

And then the triumph. We are tempted to say that such souls—or such residual puddles of what once was soul—are hardly worth damning. Yes, but the Enemy (for whatever inscrutable and perverse reason) thought them worth trying to save. Believe me, He did. You youngsters who have not yet been on active service have no idea with what labour, with what delicate skill, each of these miserable creatures was finally captured.

The difficulty lay in their very smallness and flabbiness. Here were vermin so muddled in mind, so passively responsive to environment, that it was very hard to raise them to that level of clarity and deliberateness at which mortal sin becomes possible. To raise them just enough; but not that fatal millimetre of "too much." For then of course all would possibly have been lost. They might have seen; they might have repented. On the other hand, if they had been raised too little, they would very possibly have qualified for Limbo, as creatures suitable neither for Heaven nor for Hell; things that, having failed to make the grade, are allowed to sink into a more or less contented sub-humanity forever.

In each individual choice of what the Enemy would call the "wrong" turning such creatures are at first hardly, if at all, in a state of full spiritual responsibility. They do not understand either the source or the real character of the prohibitions they are breaking. Their consciousness hardly exists apart from the social atmosphere that surrounds them. And of course we have contrived that their very language should be all smudge and blur; what would be a *bribe* in someone else's profession is a *tip* or a *present* in theirs. The job of their Tempters was first, of course, to harden these choices of the Hell-ward roads into a habit by steady repetition. But then (and this was all-important) to turn the habit into a principle—a principle the creature is prepared to defend. After that, all will go well. Conformity to the social environment, at first merely instinctive or even mechanical—how should a *jelly* not conform?—now becomes an unacknowledged creed or ideal of Togetherness or Being like Folks. Mere ignorance of the law they break now turns into a vague theory about it—remember they know no history—a theory expressed by calling it *conventional* or *puritan* or *bourgeois* "morality." Thus gradually there comes to exist at the centre of the creature a hard, tight, settled core of resolution to go on being what it is, and even to resist moods that might tend to alter it. It is a very small core; not at all reflective (they are too ignorant) nor defiant (their emotional and imaginative poverty excludes that); almost, in its own way, prim and demure; like a pebble, or a very young cancer. But it will serve our turn. Here at last is a real and deliberate, though not fully articulate, rejection of what the Enemy calls Grace.

These, then, are two welcome phenomena. First, the abundance of our captures; however tasteless our fare, we are in no danger of famine. And secondly, the triumph; the skill of our Tempters has never stood higher. But the third moral, which I have not yet drawn, is the most important of all.

The sort of souls on whose despair and ruin we have —well, I won't say feasted, but at any rate subsisted— tonight are increasing in numbers and will continue to increase. Our advices from Lower Command assure us that this is so; our directives warn us to orient all our tactics in view of this situation. The "great" sinners, those in whom vivid and genial passions have been pushed beyond the bounds and in whom an immense concentration of will has been devoted to objects which the Enemy abhors, will not disappear. But they will grow rarer. Our catches will be ever more numerous; but they will consist increasingly of trash—trash which we should once have thrown to Cerberus and the hellhounds as unfit for diabolical consumption. And there are two things I want you to understand about this. First, that however depressing it may seem, it is really a change for the better. And secondly, I would draw your attention to the means by which it has been brought about.

It is a change for the better. The great (and toothsome) sinners are made out of the very same material as those horrible phenomena, the great Saints. The virtual disappearance of such material may mean insipid meals for us. But is it not utter frustration and famine for the Enemy? He did not create the humans—He did not become one of them and die among them by torture —in order to produce candidates for Limbo; "failed" humans. He wanted to make Saints; gods; things like Himself. Is the dullness of your present fare not a very small price to pay for the delicious knowledge that His whole great experiment is petering out? But not only that. As the great sinners grow fewer, and the majority lose all individuality, the great sinners become far more effective agents for us. Every dictator or even demagogue—almost every film-star or crooner—can now draw tens of thousands of the human sheep with him.

They give themselves (what there is of them) to him; in him, to us. There may come a time when we shall have no need to bother about *individual* temptation at all, except for the few. Catch the bell-wether and his whole flock comes after him.

But do you realize how we have succeeded in reducing so many of the human race to the level of ciphers? This has not come about by accident. It has been our answer—and a magnificent answer it is—to one of the most serious challenges we ever had to face.

Let me recall to your minds what the human situation was in the latter half of the nineteenth century—the period at which I ceased to be a practising Tempter and was rewarded with an administrative post. The great movement towards liberty and equality among men had by then borne solid fruits and grown mature. Slavery had been abolished. The American War of Independence had been won. The French Revolution had succeeded. Religious toleration was almost everywhere on the increase. In that movement there had originally been many elements which were in our favour. Much Atheism, much Anti-Clericalism, much envy and thirst for revenge, even some (rather absurd) attempts to revive Paganism, were mixed in it. It was not easy to determine what our own attitude should be. On the one hand it was a bitter blow to us—it still is— that any sort of men who had been hungry should be fed or any who had long worn chains should have them struck off. But on the other hand, there was in the movement so much rejection of faith, so much materialism, secularism, and hatred, that we felt we were bound to encourage it.

But by the latter part of the century the situation was much simpler, and also much more ominous. In the English sector (where I saw most of my front-line service) a horrible thing had happened. The Enemy, with His usual sleight of hand, had largely appropriated this progressive or liberalizing movement and perverted it to His own ends. Very little of its old anti-Christianity remained. The dangerous phenomenon called Christian Socialism was rampant. Factory owners of the good old type who grew rich on sweated labour, instead of being assassinated by their workpeople—we could have used that—were being frowned upon by their own class. The rich were increasingly giving up their powers not in the face of revolution and compulsion, but in obedience to their own consciences. As for the poor who benefited by this, they were behaving in a most disappointing fashion. Instead of using their new liberties—as we reasonably hoped and expected—for massacre, rape, and looting, or even for perpetual intoxication, they were perversely engaged in becoming cleaner, more orderly, more thrifty, better educated, and even more virtuous. Believe me, gentledevils, the threat of something like a really healthy state of society seemed then perfectly serious.

Thanks to our Father Below the threat was averted. Our counter-attack was on two levels. On the deepest level our leaders contrived to call into full life an element which had been implicit in the movement from its earliest days. Hidden in the heart of this striving for Liberty there was also a deep hatred of personal freedom. That invaluable man Rousseau first revealed it. In his perfect democracy, you remember, only the state religion is permitted, slavery is restored, and the individual is told that he has really willed (though he didn't know it) whatever the Government tells him to do. From that starting point, *via* Hegel (another indispensable propagandist on our side) we easily contrived both the Nazi and the Communist state. Even in England we were pretty successful. I heard the other day that in that country a man could not, without a permit, cut down his own tree with his own axe, make it into planks with his own saw, and use the planks to build a tool-shed in his own garden.

Such was our counter-attack on one level. You, who are mere beginners, will not be entrusted with work of that kind. You will be attached as Tempters to private persons. Against them, or through them, our counter-attack takes a different form.

Democracy is the word with which you must lead them by the nose. The good work which our philological experts have already done in the corruption of human language makes it unnecessary to warn you that they should never be allowed to give this word a clear and definable meaning. They won't. It will never occur to them that *Democracy* is properly the name of a political system, even a system of voting, and that this has only the most remote and tenuous connection with what you are trying to sell them. Nor of course must they ever be allowed to raise Aristotle's question: whether "democratic behaviour" means the behaviour that democracies like or the behaviour that will preserve a democracy. For if they did, it could hardly fail to occur to them that these need not be the same.

You are to use the word purely as an incantation; if you like, purely for its selling power. It is a name they venerate. And of course it is connected with the political ideal that men should be equally treated. You then make a stealthy transition in their minds from this political ideal to a factual belief that all men *are* equal. Especially the man you are working on. As a result you can use the word *Democracy* to sanction in his thought the most degrading (and also the least enjoyable) of all human feelings. You can get him to practise, not only without shame but with a positive glow of self-approval, conduct which, if undefended by the magic word, would be universally derided.

The feeling I mean is of course that which prompts a man to say *I'm as good as you.*

The first and most obvious advantage is that you thus induce him to enthrone at the centre of his life a good, solid resounding lie. I don't mean merely that his statement is false in fact, that he is no more equal to everyone he meets in kindness, honesty, and good sense than in height or waist-measurement. I mean that he does not believe it himself. No man who says *I'm as good as you* believes it. He would not say it if he did. The St. Bernard never says it to the toy dog, nor the scholar to the dunce, nor the employable to the bum, nor the pretty woman to the plain. The claim to equality, outside the strictly political field, is made only by those who feel themselves to be in some way inferior. What it expresses is precisely the itching, smarting, writhing awareness of an inferiority which the patient refuses to accept.

And therefore resents. Yes, and therefore resents every kind of superiority in others; denigrates it; wishes its annihilation. Presently he suspects every mere difference of being a claim to superiority. No one must be different from himself in voice, clothes, manners, recreations, choice of food. "Here is someone who speaks English rather more clearly and euphoniously than I— it must be a vile, upstage, lah-di-dah affectation. Here's a fellow who says he doesn't like hot dogs—thinks himself too good for them no doubt. Here's a man who hasn't turned on the jukebox—he's one of those goddam highbrows and is doing it to show off. If they were honest-to-God all right Joes they'd be like me. They've no business to be different. It's undemocratic."

Now this useful phenomenon is in itself by no means new. Under the name of Envy it has been known to the humans for thousands of years. But hitherto they always regarded it as the most odious, and also the most comical, of vices. Those who were aware of feeling it felt it with shame; those who were not gave it no quarter in others. The delightful novelty of the present situation is that you can sanction it—make it respectable and even laudable—by the incantatory use of the word *democratic.*

Under the influence of this incantation those who are in any or every way inferior can labour more whole-heartedly and successfully than ever before to pull down everyone else to their own level. But that is not all. Under the same influence, those who come, or could come, nearer to a full humanity, actually draw back from it for fear of being *undemocratic*. I am credibly informed that young humans now sometimes suppress an incipient taste for classical music or good literature because it might prevent their Being Like Folks; that people who would really wish to be—and are offered the Grace which would enable them to be—honest, chaste, or temperate, refuse it. To accept might make them Different, might offend against the Way of Life, take them out of Togetherness, impair their Integration with the Group. They might (horror of horrors!) become individuals.

All is summed up in the prayer which a young female human is said to have uttered recently: "Oh God, make me a normal twentieth-century girl!" Thanks to our labours, this will mean increasingly, "Make me a minx, a moron, and a parasite."

Meanwhile, as a delightful by-product, the few (fewer every day) who will not be made Normal and Regular and Like Folks and Integrated, increasingly tend to become in reality the prigs and cranks which the rabble would in any case have believed them to be. For suspicion often creates what it suspects. ("Since, whatever I do, the neighbours are going to think me a witch, or a Communist agent, I might as well be hanged for a sheep as a lamb and become one in reality.") As a result we now have an intelligentsia which, though very small, is very useful to the cause of Hell.

But that is a mere by-product. What I want to fix your attention on is the vast, over-all movement towards the discrediting, and finally the elimination, of every kind of human excellence—moral, cultural, social, or intellectual. And is it not pretty to notice how *Democracy* (in the incantatory sense) is now doing for us the work that was once done by the most ancient Dictatorships, and by the same methods? You remember how one of the Greek Dictators (they called them "tyrants" then) sent an envoy to another Dictator to ask his advice about the principles of government. The second Dictator led the envoy into a field of grain, and there he snicked off with his cane the top of every stalk that rose an inch or so above the general level. The moral was plain. Allow no pre-eminence among your subjects. Let no man live who is wiser, or better, or more famous, or even handsomer than the mass. Cut them all down to a level; all slaves, all ciphers, all nobodies. All equals. Thus Tyrants could practise, in a sense, "democracy." But now "democracy" can do the same work without any other tyranny than her own. No one need now go through the field with a cane. The little stalks will now of themselves bite the tops off the big ones. The big ones are beginning to bite off their own in their desire to Be Like Stalks.

I have said that to secure the damnation of these little souls, these creatures that have almost ceased to be individual, is a laborious and tricky work. But if proper pains and skill are expended, you can be fairly confident of the result. The great sinners *seem* easier to catch. But then they are incalculable. After you have played them for seventy years, the Enemy may snatch them from your claws in the seventy-first. They are capable, you see, of real repentance. They are conscious of real guilt. They are, if things take the wrong turn, as ready to defy the social pressures around them for the Enemy's sake as they were to defy them for ours. It is in some ways more troublesome to track and swat an evasive wasp than to shoot, at close range, a wild elephant. But the elephant is more troublesome if you miss.

My own experience, as I have said, was mainly on the English sector, and I still get more news from it than from any other. It may be that what I am now going to say will not apply so fully to the sectors in which some of you may be operating. But you can make the necessary adjustments when you get there. Some application it will almost certainly have. If it has too little, you must labour to make the country you are dealing with more like what England already is.

In that promising land the spirit of *I'm as good as you* has already become something more than a generally social influence. It begins to work itself into their educational system. How far its operations there have gone at the present moment, I would not like to say with certainty. Nor does it matter. Once you have grasped the tendency, you can easily predict its future developments; especially as we ourselves will play our part in the developing. The basic principle of the new education is to be that dunces and idlers must not be made to feel inferior to intelligent and industrious pupils. That would be "undemocratic." These differences between the pupils—for they are obviously and nakedly *individual* differences—must be disguised. This can be done on various levels. At universities, examinations must be framed so that nearly all the students get good marks. Entrance examinations must be framed so that all, or nearly all, citizens can go to universities, whether they have any power (or wish) to profit by higher education or not. At schools, the children who are too stupid or lazy to learn languages and mathematics and elementary science can be set to doing the things that children used to do in their spare time. Let them, for example, make mud-pies and call it modelling. But all the time there must be no faintest hint that they are inferior to the children who are at work. Whatever nonsense they are engaged in must have—I believe the English already use the phrase—"parity of esteem." An even more drastic scheme is not impossible. Children who are fit to proceed to a higher class may be artificially kept back, because the others would get a *trauma*—Beelzebub, what a useful word!—by being left behind. The bright pupil thus remains democratically fettered to his own age-group throughout his school career, and a boy who would be capable of tackling Aeschylus or Dante sits listening to his coaeval's attempts to spell out A CAT SAT ON A MAT.

In a word, we may reasonably hope for the virtual abolition of education when *I'm as good as you* has fully had its way. All incentives to learn and all penalties for not learning will vanish. The few who might want to learn will be prevented; who are they to overtop their fellows? And anyway the teachers—or should I say, nurses?—will be far too busy reassuring the dunces and patting them on the back to waste any time on real teaching. We shall no longer have to plan and toil to spread imperturbable conceit and incurable ignorance among men. The little vermin themselves will do it for us.

Of course this would not follow unless all education became state education. But it will. That is part of the same movement. Penal taxes, designed for that purpose, are liquidating the Middle Class, the class who were prepared to save and spend and make sacrifices in order to have their children privately educated. The removal of this class, besides linking up with the abolition of education, is, fortunately, an inevitable effect of the spirit that says *I'm as good as you*. This was, after all, the social group which gave to the humans the overwhelming majority of their scientists, physicians, philosophers, theologians, poets, artists, composers, architects, jurists, and administrators. If ever there was a bunch of tall stalks that needed their tops knocked off, it was surely they. As an English politician remarked not long ago, "A democracy does not want great men."

It would be idle to ask of such a creature whether by *want* it meant "need" or "like." But you had better be clear. For here Aristotle's question comes up again.

We, in Hell, would welcome the disappearance of Democracy in the strict sense of that word; the political arrangement so called. Like all forms of government it often works to our advantage; but on the whole less often than other forms. And what we must realize is that "democracy" in the diabolical sense (*I'm as good as you*, Being like Folks, Togetherness) is the finest instrument we could possibly have for extirpating political Democracies from the face of the earth.

For "democracy" or the "democratic spirit" (diabolical sense) leads to a nation without great men, a nation mainly of subliterates, full of the cocksureness which flattery breeds on ignorance, and quick to snarl or whimper at the first hint of criticism. And that is what Hell wishes every democratic people to be. For when such a nation meets in conflict a nation where children have been made to work at school, where talent is placed in high posts, and where the ignorant mass are allowed no say at all in public affairs, only one result is possible.

The Democracies were surprised lately when they found that Russia had got ahead of them in science. What a delicious specimen of human blindness! If the whole tendency of their society is opposed to every sort of excellence, why did they expect their scientists to excel?

It is our function to encourage the behaviour,

the manners, the whole attitude of mind, which democracies naturally like and enjoy, because these are the very things which, if unchecked, will destroy democracy. You would almost wonder that even humans don't see it themselves. Even if they don't read Aristotle (that would be undemocratic) you would have thought the French Revolution would have taught them that the behaviour aristocrats naturally like is not the behaviour that preserves aristocracy. They might then have applied the same principle to all forms of government.

But I would not end on that note. I would not—Hell forbid!—encourage in your own minds that delusion which you must carefully foster in the minds of your human victims. I mean the delusion that the fate of nations is *in itself* more important than that of individual souls. The overthrow of free peoples and the multiplication of slave-states are for us a means (besides, of course, being fun); but the real end is the destruction of individuals. For only individuals can be saved or damned, can become sons of the Enemy or food for us. The ultimate value, for us, of any revolution, war, or famine lies in the individual anguish, treachery, hatred, rage, and despair which it may produce. *I'm as good as you* is a useful means for the destruction of democratic societies. But it has a far deeper value as an end in itself, as a state of mind which, necessarily excluding humility, charity, contentment, and all the pleasures of gratitude or admiration, turns a human being away from almost every road which might finally lead him to Heaven.

But now for the pleasantest part of my duty. It falls to my lot to propose on behalf of the guests the health of Principal Slubgob and the Tempters' Training College. Fill your glasses. What is this I see? What is this delicious bouquet I inhale? Can it be? Mr. Principal, I unsay all my hard words about the dinner. I see, and smell, that even under wartime conditions the College cellar still has a few dozen of sound old vintage *Pharisee*. Well, well, well. This is like old times. Hold it beneath your nostrils for a moment, gentledevils. Hold it up to the light. Look at those fiery streaks that writhe and tangle in its dark heart, as if they were contending. And so they are. You know how this wine is blended? Different types of Pharisee have been harvested, trodden, and fermented together to produce its subtle flavour. Types that were most antagonistic to one another on Earth. Some were all rules and relics and rosaries; others were all drab clothes, long faces, and petty traditional abstinences from wine or cards or the theatre. Both had in common their self-righteousness and the almost infinite distance between their actual outlook and anything the Enemy really is or commands. The wickedness of other religions was the really live doctrine in the religion of each; slander was its gospel and denigration its litany. How they hated each other up there where the sun shone! How much more they hate each other now that they are forever conjoined but not reconciled. Their astonishment, their resentment, at the combination, the festering of their eternally impenitent spite, passing into our spiritual digestion, will work like fire.

Dark fire. All said and done, my friends, it will be an ill day for us if what most humans mean by "religion" ever vanishes from the Earth. It can still send us the truly delicious sins. The fine flower of unholiness can grow only in the close neighbourhood of the Holy. Nowhere do we tempt so successfully as on the very steps of the altar.

Your Imminence, your Disgraces, my Thorns, Shadies, and Gentledevils: I give you the toast of—Principal Slubgob and the College!

Good works" in the plural is an expression much more familiar to modern Christendom than "good work." Good works are chiefly alms-giving or "helping" in the parish. They are quite separate from one's "work." And good works need not be good work, as anyone can see by inspecting some of the objects made to be sold at bazaars for charitable purposes. This is not according to our example. When our Lord provided a poor wedding party with an extra glass of wine all round, he was doing good works. But also good work; it was a wine really worth drinking. Nor is the neglect of goodness in our "work," our job, according to precept. The apostle says every one must not only work but work to produce what is "good."

The idea of Good Work is not quite extinct among us, though it is not, I fear, especially characteristic of religious people. I have found it among cabinet-makers, cobblers, and sailors. It is no use at all trying to impress sailors with a new liner because she is the biggest or costliest ship afloat. They look for what they call her "lines": they predict how she will behave in a heavy sea. Artists also talk of Good Work; but decreasingly. They begin to prefer words like "significant," "important," "contemporary," or "daring." These are not, to my mind, good symptoms.

But the great mass of men in all fully industrialized societies are the victims of a situation which almost excludes the idea of Good Work from the outset. "Built-in obsolescence" becomes an economic necessity. Unless an article is so made that it will go to pieces in a year or two and thus have to be replaced, you will not get a sufficient turnover. A hundred years ago, when a man got married, he had built for him (if he were rich enough) a carriage in which he expected to drive for the rest of his life. He now buys a car which he expects to sell again in two years. Work nowadays must *not* be good.

For the wearer, zip fasteners have this advantage over buttons: that, while they last, they will save him an infinitesimal amount of time and trouble. For the producer, they have a much more solid merit; they don't remain in working order long. Bad work is the *desideratum.*

We must avoid taking a glibly moral view of this situation. It is not solely the result of original or actual sin. It has stolen upon us, unforeseen and unintended. The degraded commercialism of our minds is quite as much its result as its cause. Nor can it, in my opinion, be cured by purely moral efforts.

Originally things are made for use, or delight, or (more often) for both. The savage hunter makes himself a weapon of flint or bone; makes it as well as he can, for if it is blunt or brittle he will kill no meat. His woman makes a clay pot to fetch water in; again as well as she can, for she will have to use it. But they do not for long (if at all) abstain from decorating these things; they want to have (like Dogberry) "everything handsome about them." And while they work, we may be sure they sing or whistle or at least hum. They may tell stories too.

Into this situation, unobtrusive as Eden's snake and at first as innocent as that snake once was, there must sooner or later come a change. Each family no longer makes all it needs. There is a specialist, a potter making pots for the whole village; a smith making weapons for all; a bard (poet and musician in one) singing and story-telling for all. It is significant that in Homer the smith of the gods is lame, and the poet among men is blind. That may be how the thing began. The defectives, who are no use as hunters or warriors, may be set aside to provide both necessaries and recreation for those who are.

The importance of this change is that we now have people making things (pots, swords, lays) not for their own use and delight but for the use and delight of others. And of course they must, in some way or other, be rewarded for doing it. The change is necessary unless society and arts are to remain in a state not of paradisal, but of feeble, blundering, and impoverishing simplicity. It is kept healthy by two facts. First, these specialists will do their work as well as they can. They are right up against the people who are going to use it. You'll have all the women in the village after you if you make bad pots. You'll be shouted down if you sing a dull lay. If you make bad swords, then at best the warriors will come back and thrash you; at worst, they won't come back at all, for the enemy will have killed them, and your village will be burned and you yourself enslaved or knocked on the head. And secondly, because the specialists are doing as well as they can something that is indisputably worth doing, they will delight in their work. We must not idealise. It will not all be delight. The smith may be overworked. The bard may be frustrated when the village insists on hearing his last lay over again (or a new one exactly like it) while he is longing to get a hearing for some wonderful innovation. But, by and large, the specialists have a life fit for a man; usefulness, a reasonable amount of honour, and the joy of exercising skill.

I lack space and, of course, knowledge, to trace the whole process from this state of affairs to that in which we are living to-day. But I think we can now disengage the essence of the change. Granted the departure from the primitive condition in which every one makes things for himself, and granted, therefore, a condition in which many work for others (who will pay them), there are still two sorts of job. Of one sort, a man can truly say, "I am doing work which is worth doing. It would still be worth doing if nobody paid for it. But as I have no private means, and need to be fed and housed and clothed, I must be paid while I do it." The other kind of job is that in which people do work whose sole purpose is the earning of money; work which need not be, ought not to be, or would not be, done by anyone in the whole world unless it were paid.

We may thank God there are still plenty of jobs in the first category. The agricultural labourer, the policeman, the doctor, the artist, the teacher, the priest, and many others, are doing what is worth doing in itself; what quite a number of people would do, and do, without pay; what every family would attempt to do for itself, in some amateurish fashion, if it lived in primitive isolation. Of course jobs of this kind need not be agreeable. Ministering to a leper settlement is one of them.

The opposite extreme may be represented by two examples. I do not necessarily equate them morally, but they are alike by our present classification. One is the work of the professional prostitute. The peculiar horror of her work—if you say we should not call it work, think again—the thing that makes it so much more horrible than ordinary fornication, is that it is an extreme example of an activity which has no possible end in view except money. You cannot go further in that direction than sexual intercourse, not only without marriage, not only without love, but even without lust. My other example is this. I often see a hoarding which bears a notice to the effect that thousands look at this space and your firm ought to hire it for an advertisement of its wares. Consider by how many stages this is separated from "making that which is good." A carpenter has made this hoarding; that, in itself, has no use.

75

Printers and paper-makers have worked to produce the notice—worthless until someone hires the space—worthless to him until he pastes on it another notice, still worthless to him unless it persuades someone else to buy his goods; which themselves may well be ugly, useless, and pernicious luxuries that no mortal would have bought unless the advertisement, by its sexy or snobbish incantations, had conjured up in him a factitious desire for them. At every stage of the process, work is being done whose sole value lies in the money it brings.

Such would seem to be the inevitable result of a society which depends predominantly on buying and selling. In a rational world, things would be made because they were wanted; in the actual world, wants have to be created in order that people may receive money for making the things. That is why the distrust or contempt of trade which we find in earlier societies should not be too hastily set down as mere snobbery. The more important trade is, the more people are condemned to—and, worse still, learn to prefer—what we have called the second kind of job. Work worth doing apart from its pay, enjoyable work, and good work become the privilege of a fortunate minority. The competitive search for customers dominates international situations.

Within my lifetime in England money was (very properly) collected to buy shirts for some men who were out of work. The work they were out of was the manufacture of shirts.

That such a state of affairs cannot be permanent is easily foreseen. But unfortunately it is most likely to perish by its own internal contradictions in a manner which will cause immense suffering. It can be ended painlessly only if we find some way of ending it voluntarily; and needless to say I have no plan for doing that, and none of our masters—the Big Men behind government and industry—would take any notice if I had. The only hopeful sign at the moment is the "space-race" between America and Russia. Since we have got ourselves into a state where the main problem is not to provide people with what they need or like, but to keep people making things (it hardly matters what), great powers could not easily be better employed than in fabricating costly objects which they then fling overboard. It keeps money circulating and factories working, and it won't do space much harm—or not for a long time. But the relief is partial and temporary. The main practical task for most of us is not to give the Big Men advice about how to end our fatal economy—we have none to give and they wouldn't listen—but to consider how we can live within it as little hurt and degraded as possible.

It is something even to recognize that it is fatal and insane. Just as the Christian has a great advantage over other men, not by being less fallen than they nor less doomed to live in a fallen world, but by knowing that he *is* a fallen man in a fallen world; so we shall do better if we remember at every moment what Good Work was and how impossible it has now become for the majority. We may have to earn our living by taking part in the production of objects which are rotten in quality and which, even if they were good in quality, would not be worth producing—the demand or "market" for them having been simply engineered by advertisement. Beside the waters of Babylon—or the assembly belt— we shall still say inwardly, "If I forget thee, O Jerusalem, may my right hand forget its cunning." (It will.)

And of course we shall keep our eyes skinned for any chance of escape. If we have any "choice of a career" (but has one man in a thousand any such thing?) we shall be after the sane jobs like greyhounds and stick there like limpets. We shall try, if we get the chance, to earn our living by doing well what would be worth doing even if we had not our living to earn. A considerable mortification of our avarice may be necessary. It is usually the insane jobs that lead to big money; they are often also the least laborious.

But beyond all this there is something subtler. We must take great care to preserve our habits of mind from infection by those which the situation has bred. Such an infection has, in my opinion, deeply corrupted our artists.

Until quite recently—until the latter part of the last century—it was taken for granted that the business of the artist was to delight and instruct his public. There were, of course, different publics; the street-songs and the oratorios were not addressed to the same audience (though I think a good many people liked both). And an artist might lead his public on to appreciate finer things than they had wanted at first; but he could do this only by being, from the first, if not merely entertaining, yet entertaining, and if not completely intelligible, yet very largely intelligible. All this has changed. In the highest aesthetic circles one now hears nothing about the artist's duty to us. It is all about our duty to him. He owes us nothing; we owe him "recognition," even though he has never paid the slightest attention to our tastes, interests, or habits. If we don't give it to him, our name is mud. In this shop, the customer is always wrong.

But this change is surely part of our changed attitude to all work. As "giving employment" becomes more important than making things men need or like, there is a tendency to regard every trade as something that exists chiefly for the sake of those who practise it. The smith does not work in order that the warriors may fight; the warriors exist and fight in order that the smith may be kept busy. The bard does not exist in order to delight the tribe; the tribe exists in order to appreciate the bard.

In industry highly creditable motives, as well as insanity, lie behind this change of attitude. A real advance in charity stopped us talking about "surplus population" and started us talking instead about "unemployment." The danger is that this should lead us to forget that employment is not an end in itself. We want people to be employed only as a means to their being fed—believing (whether rightly, who knows?) that it is better to feed them even for making bad things badly than for doing nothing.

But though we have a duty to feed the hungry, I doubt whether we have a duty to "appreciate" the ambitious. This attitude to art is fatal to good work. Many modern novels, poems, and pictures, which we are brow-beaten into "appreciating," are not good work because they are not *work* at all. They are mere puddles of spilled sensibility or reflection. When an artist is in the strict sense working, he of course takes into account the existing taste, interests, and capacity of his audience. These, no less than the language, the marble, or the paint, are part of his raw material; to be used, tamed, sublimated, not ignored nor defied. Haughty indifference to them is not genius nor integrity; it is laziness and incompetence. You have not learned your job. Hence, real honest-to-God work, so far as the arts are concerned, now appears chiefly in low-brow art; in the film, the detective story, the children's story. These are often sound structures; seasoned wood, accurately dovetailed, the stresses all calculated; skill and labour successfully used to do what is intended. Do not misunderstand. The high-brow productions may, of course, reveal a finer sensibility and profounder thought. But a puddle is not a work, whatever rich wines or oils or medicines have gone into it.

"Great works" (of art) and "good works" (of charity) had better also be Good Work. Let choirs sing well or not at all. Otherwise we merely confirm the majority in their conviction that the world of Business, which does with such efficiency so much that never really needed doing, is the real, the adult, and the practical world; and that all this "culture" and all this "religion" (horrid words both) are essentially marginal, amateurish, and rather effeminate activities.

I<small>N</small> my time I have heard two quite different arguments against my religion put forward in the name of science. When I was a youngster, people used to say that the universe was not only not friendly to life but positively hostile to it. Life had appeared on this planet by a millionth chance, as if at one point there had been a breakdown of the elaborate defenses generally enforced against it. We should be rash to assume that such a leak had occurred more than once. Probably life was a purely terrestrial abnormality. We were alone in an infinite desert. Which just showed the absurdity of the Christian idea that there was a Creator who was interested in living creatures.

But then came Professor F. B. Hoyle, the Cambridge cosmologist, and in a fortnight or so everyone I met seemed to have decided that the universe was probably quite well provided with inhabitable globes and with livestock to inhabit them. Which just showed (equally well) the absurdity of Christianity with its parochial idea that Man could be important to God.

This is a warning of what we may expect if we ever do discover animal life (vegetable does not matter) on another planet. Each new discovery, even every new theory, is held at first to have the most wide-reaching theological and philosophical consequences. It is seized by unbelievers as the basis for a new attack on Christianity; it is often, and more embarrassingly, seized by injudicious believers as the basis for a new defence.

But usually, when the popular hubbub has subsided and the novelty has been chewed over by real theologians, real scientists and real philosophers, both sides find themselves pretty much where they were before. So it was with Copernican astronomy, with Darwinism, with Biblical Criticism, with the new psychology. So, I cannot help expecting, it will be with the discovery of "life on other planets"—if that discovery is ever made.

The supposed threat is clearly directed against the doctrine of the Incarnation, the belief that God of God "for us men and for our salvation came down from heaven and was . . . made man." Why for us men more than for others? If we find ourselves to be but one among a million races, scattered through a million spheres, how can we, without absurd arrogance, believe ourselves to have been uniquely favored? I admit that the question could become formidable. In fact, it will become formidable when, if ever, we know the answer to five other questions.

1. Are there animals anywhere except on earth? We do not know. We do not know whether we ever shall know.

84

2. Supposing there were, have any of these animals what we call "rational souls"? By this I include not merely the faculty to abstract and calculate, but the apprehension of values, the power to mean by "good" something more than "good for me" or even "good for my species." If instead of asking, "Have they rational souls?" you prefer to ask, "Are they spiritual animals?" I think we shall both mean pretty much the same. If the answer to either question should be No, then of course it would not be at all strange that our species should be treated differently from theirs.

There would be no sense in offering to a creature, however clever or amiable, a gift which that creature was by its nature incapable either of desiring or of receiving. We teach our sons to read but not our dogs. The dogs prefer bones. And of course, since we do not yet know whether there are extra-terrestrial animals at all, we are a long way from knowing that they are rational (or "spiritual").

Even if we met them we might not find it so easy to decide. It seems to me possible to suppose creatures so clever that they could talk, though they were, from the theological point of view, really only animals, capable of pursuing or enjoying only natural ends. One meets humans—the machine-minded and materialistic urban type—who *look* as if they were just that. As Christians we must believe the appearance to be false; somewhere under that glib surface there lurks, however atrophied, a human soul. But in other worlds there might be things that really are what these seem to be. Conversely, there might be creatures genuinely spiritual, whose powers of manufacture and abstract thought were so humble that we should mistake them for mere animals. God shield them from us!

3. If there are species, and rational species, other than man, are any or all of them, like us, fallen? This is the point non-Christians always seem to forget. They seem to think that the Incarnation implies some particular merit or excellence in humanity. But of course it implies just the reverse: a particular demerit and depravity. No creature that deserved Redemption would need to be redeemed. They that are whole need not the physician. Christ died for men precisely because men are *not* worth dying for; to make them worth it. Notice what waves of utterly unwarranted hypothesis these critics of Christianity want us to swim through. We are now supposing the fall of hypothetically rational creatures whose mere existence is hypothetical!

4. If all of them (and surely *all* is a long shot) or any of them have fallen have they been denied Redemption by the Incarnation and Passion of Christ? For of course it is no very new idea that the eternal Son may, for all we know, have been incarnate in other worlds than earth and so saved other races than ours. As Alice Meynell wrote in "Christ in the Universe":

> . . . *in the eternities*
> *Doubtless we shall compare together, hear*
> *A million alien Gospels, in what guise*
> *He trod the Pleiades, the Lyre, the Bear.*

86

I wouldn't go as far as "doubtless" myself. Perhaps of all races *we* only fell. Perhaps Man is the only lost sheep; the one, therefore, whom the Shepherd came to seek. Or perhaps—but this brings us to the next wave of assumption. It is the biggest yet and will knock us head over heels, but I am fond of a tumble in the surf.

5. If we knew (which we don't) the answers to 1, 2, and 3—and, further, if we knew that Redemption by an Incarnation and Passion had been denied to creatures in need of it—is it certain that this is the only mode of Redemption that is possible? Here of course we ask for what is not merely unknown but, unless God should reveal it, wholly unknowable. It may be that the further we were permitted to see into His councils, the more clearly we should understand that thus and not otherwise—by the birth at Bethlehem, the cross on Calvary and the empty tomb—a fallen race could be rescued. There may be a necessity for this, insurmountable, rooted in the very nature of God and the very nature of sin. But we don't know. At any rate, I don't know. Spiritual as well as physical conditions might differ widely in different worlds. There might be different sorts and different degrees of fallenness. We must surely believe that the divine charity is as fertile in resource as it is measureless in condescension. To different diseases, or even to different patients sick with the same disease, the great Physician may have applied different remedies; remedies which we should probably not recognize as such even if we ever heard of them.

It might turn out that the redemption of other species

differed from ours by working through ours. There is a hint of something like this in St. Paul (Romans 8:19-23) when he says that the whole creation is longing and waiting to be delivered from some kind of slavery, and that the deliverance will occur only when we, we Christians, fully enter upon our sonship to God and exercise our "glorious liberty."

On the conscious level I believe that he was thinking only of our own Earth: of animal, and probably vegetable, life on Earth being "renewed" or glorified at the glorification of man in Christ. But it is perhaps possible —it is not necessary—to give his words a cosmic meaning. It may be that Redemption, starting with us, is to work from us and through us.

This would no doubt give man a pivotal position. But such a position need not imply any superiority in us or any favouritism in God. The general, deciding where to begin his attack, does not select the prettiest landscape or the most fertile field or the most attractive village. Christ was not born in a stable because a stable is, in itself, the most convenient or distinguished place for a maternity.

Only if we had some such function would a contact between us and such unknown races be other than a calamity. If indeed we were unfallen, it would be another matter.

It sets one dreaming—to interchange thoughts with beings whose thinking had an organic background wholly different from ours (other senses, other appetites), to be unenviously humbled by intellects possibly superior to our own yet able for that very reason to descend to our level, to descend lovingly ourselves if we met innocent and childlike creatures who could never be as strong or as clever as we, to exchange with the inhabitants of other worlds that especially keen and rich affection which exists between unlikes; it is a glorious dream. But make no mistake. It *is* a dream. We are fallen.

We know what our race does to strangers. Man destroys or enslaves every species he can. Civilized man murders, enslaves, cheats, and corrupts savage man. Even inanimate nature he turns into dust bowls and slag-heaps. There are individuals who don't. But they are not the sort who are likely to be our pioneers in space. Our ambassador to new worlds will be the needy and greedy adventurer or the ruthless technical expert. They will do as their kind has always done. What that will be if they meet things weaker than themselves, the black man and the red man can tell. If they meet things stronger, they will be, very properly, destroyed.

It is interesting to wonder how things would go if they met an unfallen race. At first, to be sure, they'd have a grand time jeering at, duping, and exploiting its innocence; but I doubt if our half-animal cunning would long be a match for godlike wisdom, selfless valour, and perfect unanimity.

I therefore fear the practical, not the theoretical, problems which will arise if ever we meet rational creatures which are not human. Against them we shall, if we can, commit all the crimes we have already committed against creatures certainly human but differing from us in features and pigmentation; and the starry heavens will become an object to which good men can look up only with feelings of intolerable guilt, agonized pity, and burning shame.

Of course after the first debauch of exploitation we shall make some belated attempt to do better. We shall perhaps send missionaries. But can even missionaries be trusted? "Gun and gospel" have been horribly combined in the past. The missionary's holy desire to save souls has not always been kept quite distinct from the arrogant desire, the busybody's itch, to (as he calls it) "civilize" the (as he calls them) "natives." Would all our missionaries recognize an unfallen race if they met it? Could they? Would they continue to press upon creatures that did not need to be saved that plan of Salvation which God has appointed for Man? Would they denounce as sins mere differences of behaviour which the spiritual and biological history of these strange creatures fully justified and which God Himself had blessed? Would they try to teach those from whom they had better learn? I do not know.

What I do know is that here and now, as our only possible practical preparation for such a meeting, you and I should resolve to stand firm against all exploitation and all theological imperialism. It will not be fun. We shall be called traitors to our own species. We shall be hated of almost all men; even of some religious men. And we must not give back one single inch. We shall probably fail, but let us go down fighting for the right side. Our loyalty is due not to our species but to God. Those who are, or can become, His sons, are our real brothers even if they have shells or tusks. It is spiritual, not biological, kinship that counts.

But let us thank God that we are still very far from travel to other worlds.

I have wondered before now whether the vast astronomical distances may not be God's quarantine precautions. They prevent the spiritual infection of a fallen species from spreading. And of course we are also very far from the supposed theological problem which contact with other rational species might raise. Such species may not exist. There is not at present a shred of empirical evidence that they do. There is nothing but what the logicians would call arguments from "*a priori* probability"—arguments that begin "It is only natural to suppose," or "All analogy suggests," or "Is it not the height of arrogance to rule out—?" They make very good reading. But who except a born gambler ever risks five dollars on such grounds in ordinary life?

And, as we have seen, the mere existence of these creatures would not raise a problem. After that, we still need to know that they are fallen; then, that they have not been, or will not be, redeemed in the mode we know; and then, that no other mode is possible. I think a Christian is sitting pretty if his faith never encounters more formidable difficulties than these conjectural phantoms.

If I remember rightly, St. Augustine raised a question about the theological position of satyrs, monopods, and other semi-human creatures. He decided it could wait till we knew there were any. So can this.

"But supposing," you say. "Supposing all these embarrassing suppositions turned out to be true?" I can only record a conviction that they won't; a conviction which has for me become in the course of years irresistible. Christians and their opponents again and again expect that some new discovery will either turn matters of faith into matters of knowledge or else reduce them to patent absurdities. But it has never happened.

What we believe always remains intellectually possible; it never becomes intellectually compulsive. I have an idea that when this ceases to be so, the world will be ending. We have been warned that *all but* conclusive evidence against Christianity, evidence that would deceive (if it were possible) the very elect, will appear with Antichrist.

And after that there will be wholly conclusive evidence on the other side.

But not, I fancy, till then on either side.

THERE are many reasons why the modern Christian and even the modern theologian may hesitate to give to the doctrine of Christ's Second Coming that emphasis which was usually laid on it by our ancestors. Yet it seems to me impossible to retain in any recognisable form our belief in the Divinity of Christ and the truth of the Christian revelation while abandoning, or even persistently neglecting, the promised, and threatened, Return. "He shall come again to judge the quick and the dead," says the Apostles' Creed. "This same Jesus," said the angels in Acts, "shall so come in like manner as ye have seen him go into heaven." "Hereafter," said our Lord himself (by those words inviting crucifixion), "shall ye see the Son of Man . . . coming in the clouds of heaven." If this is not an integral part of the faith once given to the saints, I do not know what is. In the following pages I shall endeavour to deal with some of the thoughts that may deter modern men from a firm belief in, or a due attention to, the return or Second Coming of the Saviour. I have no claim to speak as an expert in any of the studies involved, and merely put forward the reflections which have arisen in my own mind and have seemed to me (perhaps wrongly) to be helpful. They are all submitted to the correction of wiser heads.

The grounds for modern embarrassment about this doctrine fall into two groups, which may be called the theoretical and the practical. I will deal with the theoretical first.

Many are shy of this doctrine because they are reacting (in my opinion very properly reacting) against a school of thought which is associated with the great name of Dr. Albert Schweitzer. According to that school, Christ's teaching about his own return and the end of the world—what theologians call his "apocalyptic"— was the very essence of his message. All his other doctrines radiated from it; his moral teaching everywhere presupposed a speedy end of the world. If pressed to an extreme, this view, as I think Chesterton said, amounts to seeing in Christ little more than an earlier William Miller, who created a local "scare." I am not saying that Dr. Schweitzer pressed it to that conclusion: but it has seemed to some that his thought invites us in that direction. Hence, from fear of that extreme, arises a tendency to soft-pedal what Schweitzer's school has overemphasized.

For my own part I hate and distrust reactions not only in religion but in everything. Luther surely spoke very good sense when he compared humanity to a drunkard who, after falling off his horse on the right, falls off it next time on the left. I am convinced that those who find in Christ's apocalyptic the whole of his message are mistaken. But a thing does not vanish—it is not even discredited—because someone has spoken of it with exaggeration. It remains exactly where it was. The only difference is that if it has recently been exaggerated, we must now take special care not to overlook it; for that is the side on which the drunk man is now most likely to fall off.

The very name "apocalyptic" assigns our Lord's predictions of the Second Coming to a class. There are other specimens of it: the *Apocalypse of Baruch*, the *Book of Enoch*, or the *Ascension of Isaiah*. Christians are far from regarding such texts as Holy Scripture, and to most modern tastes the *genre* appears tedious and unedifying. Hence there arises a feeling that our Lord's predictions, being "much the same sort of thing," are discredited. The charge against them might be put either in a harsher or a gentler form. The harsher form would run, in the mouth of an atheist, something like this: "You see that, after all, your vaunted Jesus was really the same sort of crank or charlatan as all the other writers of apocalyptic." The gentler form, used more probably by a modernist, would be like this: "Every great man is partly of his own age and partly for all time. What matters in his work is always that which transcends his age, not that which he shared with a thousand forgotten contemporaries. We value Shakespeare for the glory of his language and his knowledge of the human heart, which were his own; not for his belief in witches or the divine right of kings, or his failure to take a daily bath. So with Jesus. His belief in a speedy and catastrophic end to history belongs to him not as a great teacher but as a first-century Palestinian peasant. It was one of his inevitable limitations, best forgotten. We must concentrate on what distinguished him from other first-century Palestinian peasants, on his moral and social teaching."

As an argument against the reality of the Second Coming this seems to me to beg the question at issue. When we propose to ignore in a great man's teaching those doctrines which it has in common with the thought of his age, we seem to be assuming that the thought of his age was erroneous. When we select for serious consideration those doctrines which "transcend" the thought of his own age and are "for all time," we are assuming that the thought of *our* age is correct: for of course by thoughts which transcend the great man's age we really mean thoughts that agree with ours. Thus I value Shakespeare's picture of the transformation in old Lear more than I value his views about the divine right of kings, because I agree with Shakespeare that a man can be purified by suffering like Lear, but do not believe that kings (or any other rulers) have divine right in the sense required. When the great man's views do not seem to us erroneous we do not value them the less for having been shared with his contemporaries. Shakespeare's disdain for treachery and Christ's blessing on the poor were not alien to the outlook of their respective periods; but no one wishes to discredit them on that account. No one would reject Christ's apocalyptic on the ground that apocalyptic was common in first-century Palestine unless he had already decided that the thought of first-century Palestine was in that respect mistaken. But to have so decided is surely to have begged the question; for the question is whether the expectation of a catastrophic and Divinely ordered end of the present universe is true or false.

If we have an open mind on that point, the whole problem is altered. If such an end is really going to occur, and if (as is the case) the Jews had been trained by their religion to expect it, then it is very natural that they should produce apocalyptic literature. On that view, our Lord's production of something like the other apocalyptic documents would not necessarily result from his supposed bondage to the errors of his period, but would be the Divine exploitation of a sound element in contemporary Judaism: nay, the time and place in which it pleased him to be incarnate would, presumably, have been chosen because, there and then, that element existed, and had, by his eternal providence, been developed for that very purpose. For if we once accept the doctrine of the Incarnation, we must surely be very cautious in suggesting that any circumstance in the culture of first-century Palestine was a hampering or distorting influence upon his teaching. Do we suppose that the scene of God's earthly life was selected at random?—that some other scene would have served better?

But there is worse to come. "Say what you like," we shall be told, "the apocalyptic beliefs of the first Christians have been proved to be false. It is clear from the New Testament that they all expected the Second Coming in their own lifetime. And, worse still, they had a reason, and one which you will find very embarrassing. Their Master had told them so. He shared, and indeed created, their delusion. He said in so many words, 'this generation shall not pass till all these things be done.' And he was wrong. He clearly knew no more about the end of the world than anyone else."

It is certainly the most embarrassing verse in the Bible. Yet how teasing, also, that within fourteen words of it should come the statement "But of that day and that hour knoweth no man, no, not the angels which are in heaven, neither the Son, but the Father." The one exhibition of error and the one confession of ignorance grow side by side. That they stood thus in the mouth of Jesus himself, and were not merely placed thus by the reporter, we surely need not doubt. Unless the reporter were perfectly honest he would never have recorded the confession of ignorance at all; he could have had no motive for doing so except a desire to tell the whole truth. And unless later copyists were equally honest they would never have preserved the (apparently) mistaken prediction about "this generation" after the passage of time had shown the (apparent) mistake. This passage (Mark 13:30-32) and the cry "Why hast thou forsaken me?" (Mark 15:34) together make up the strongest proof that the New Testament is historically reliable. The evangelists have the first great characteris-

THE WORLD'S LAST NIGHT

tic of honest witnesses: they mention facts which are, at first sight, damaging to their main contention.

The facts, then, are these: that Jesus professed himself (in some sense) ignorant, and within a moment showed that he really was so. To believe in the Incarnation, to believe that he is God, makes it hard to understand how he could be ignorant; but also makes it certain that, if he said he could be ignorant, then ignorant he could really be. For a God who can be ignorant is less baffling than a God who falsely professes ignorance. The answer of theologians is that the God-Man was omniscient as God, and ignorant as Man. This, no doubt, is true, though it cannot be imagined. Nor indeed can the unconsciousness of Christ in sleep be imagined, nor the twilight of reason in his infancy; still less his merely organic life in his mother's womb. But the physical sciences, no less than theology, propose for our belief much that cannot be imagined.

A generation which has accepted the curvature of space need not boggle at the impossibility of imagining the consciousness of incarnate God. In that consciousness the temporal and the timeless were united. I think we can acquiesce in mystery at that point, provided we do not aggravate it by our tendency to picture the timeless life of God as, simply, another sort of time. We are committing that blunder whenever we ask how Christ could be *at the same moment* ignorant and omniscient, or how he could be the God who neither slumbers nor sleeps *while* he slept. The italicized

words conceal an attempt to establish a temporal relation between his timeless life as God and the days,
months, and years of his life as Man. And of course
there is no such relation. The Incarnation is not an epi-
sode in the life of God: the Lamb is slain—and therefore presumably born, grown to maturity, and risen—
from all eternity. The taking up into God's nature of
humanity, with all its ignorances and limitations, is
not itself a temporal event, though the humanity which
is so taken up was, like our own, a thing living and dying in time. And if limitation, and therefore ignorance,
was thus taken up, we ought to expect that the ignorance
should at some time be actually displayed. It would be
difficult, and, to me, repellent, to suppose that Jesus
never asked a genuine question, that is, a question to
which he did not know the answer. That would make of
his humanity something so unlike ours as scarcely to de-
serve the name. I find it easier to believe that when he
said "Who touched me?" (Luke 7:45) he really wanted
to know.

The difficulties which I have so far discussed are, to a
certain extent, debating points. They tend rather to
strengthen a disbelief already based on other grounds
than to create disbelief by their own force. We are now
coming to something much more important and often
less fully conscious. The doctrine of the Second Coming is deeply uncongenial to the whole evolutionary or
developmental character of modern thought. We have
been taught to think of the world as something that
grows slowly towards perfection, something that "pro-

gresses" or "evolves." Christian Apocalyptic offers us no such hope. It does not even foretell (which would be more tolerable to our habits of thought) a gradual decay. It foretells a sudden, violent end imposed from without; an extinguisher popped onto the candle, a brick flung at the gramophone, a curtain rung down on the play—"Halt!"

To this deep-seated objection I can only reply that, in my opinion, the modern conception of Progress or Evolution (as popularly imagined) is simply a myth, supported by no evidence whatever.

I say "evolution, as popularly imagined." I am not in the least concerned to refute Darwinism as a theorem in biology. There may be flaws in that theorem, but I have here nothing to do with them. There may be signs that biologists are already contemplating a withdrawal from the whole Darwinian position, but I claim to be no judge of such signs. It can even be argued that what Darwin really accounted for was not the origin, but the elimination, of species, but I will not pursue that argument. For purposes of this article I am assuming that Darwinian biology is correct. What I want to point out is the illegitimate transition from the Darwinian theorem in biology to the modern myth of evolutionism or developmentalism or progress in general.

The first thing to notice is that the myth arose earlier than the theorem, in advance of all evidence. Two great works of art embody the idea of a universe in which, by some inherent necessity, the "higher" always supersedes the "lower." One is Keats's *Hyperion* and the other is

Wagner's *Nibelung's Ring*. And they are both earlier
than the *Origin of Species*. You could not have a clearer
expression of the developmental or progressive idea
than Oceanus' words

> 'tis the eternal law
> *That first in beauty should be first in might.*

And you could not have a more ardent submission to it
than those words in which Wagner describes his
tetralogy.

> *The progress of the whole poem, therefore [he writes
> to Röckel in 1854], shows the necessity of recognising,
> and submitting to, the change, the diversity, the multi-
> plicity, and the eternal novelty, of the Real. Wotan rises
> to the tragic heights of willing his own downfall. This
> is all that we have to learn from the history of Man—
> to will the Necessary, and ourselves to bring it to pass.
> The creative work which this highest and self-renounc-
> ing will finally accomplishes is the fearless and ever-
> loving man, Siegfried.* *

> * "*Der Fortgang des ganzen Gedichtes zeigt demnach die Notwen-
> digkeit, den Wechsel, die Mannigfaltigkeit, die Vielheit, die ewige
> Neuheit der Wirklichkeit und des Lebens anzuerkennen und ihr zu
> weichen. Wotan schwingt sich bis zu der tragischen Höhe, seinen
> Untergang zu wollen. Dies ist alles, was wir aus der Geschichte der
> Menscheit zu lernen haben: das Notwendige zu wollen und selbst zu
> vollbringen. Das Schöpfungswerk dieses höchsten, selbst vernichtenden
> Willens ist der endlich gewonnene furchtlose, stets liebende Mensch;
> Siegfried.*"

Fuller research into the origins of this potent myth would lead us
to the German idealists and thence (as I have heard suggested) through
Boehme back to Alchemy. Is the whole dialectical view of history possibly a gigantic projection of the old dream that we can make gold?

The idea that the myth (so potent in all modern thought) is a result of Darwin's biology would thus seem to be unhistorical. On the contrary, the attraction of Darwinism was that it gave to a pre-existing myth the scientific reassurances it required. If no evidence for evolution had been forthcoming, it would have been necessary to invent it. The real sources of the myth are partly political. It projects onto the cosmic screen feelings engendered by the Revolutionary period.

In the second place, we must notice that Darwinism gives no support to the belief that natural selection, working upon chance variations, has a general tendency to produce improvement. The illusion that it has comes from confining our attention to a few species which have (by some possibly arbitrary standard of our own) changed for the better. Thus the horse has improved in the sense that *protohippos* would be less useful to us than his modern descendant. The anthropoid has improved in the sense that he now is Ourselves. But a great many of the changes produced by evolution are not improvements by any conceivable standard. In battle men save their lives sometimes by advancing and sometimes by retreating. So, in the battle for survival, species save themselves sometimes by increasing, sometimes by jettisoning, their powers. There is no general law of progress in biological history.

And, thirdly, even if there were, it would not follow —it is, indeed, manifestly not the case—that there is any law of progress in ethical, cultural, and social history. No one looking at world history without some preconception in favor of progress could find in it a steady up gradient. There is often progress within a given field over a limited period. A school of pottery or painting, a moral effort in a particular direction, a practical art like sanitation or shipbuilding, may continuously improve over a number of years. If this process could spread to all departments of life and continue indefinitely, there would be "Progress" of the sort our fathers believed in. But it never seems to do so. Either it is interrupted (by barbarian irruption or the even less resistible infiltration of modern industrialism) or else, more mysteriously, it decays. The idea which here shuts out the Second Coming from our minds, the idea of the world slowly ripening to perfection, is a myth, not a generalization from experience. And it is a myth which distracts us from our real duties and our real interest. It is our attempt to guess the plot of a drama in which we are the characters. But how can the characters in a play guess the plot? We are not the playwright, we are not the producer, we are not even the audience. We are on the stage. To play well the scenes in which we are "on" concerns us much more than to guess about the scenes that follow it.

In *King Lear* (III:vii) there is a man who is such a minor character that Shakespeare has not given him even a name: he is merely "First Servant." All the characters around him—Regan, Cornwall, and Edmund—have fine long-term plans. They think they know how the story is going to end, and they are quite wrong. The servant has no such delusions. He has no notion how the play is going to go. But he understands the present scene. He sees an abomination (the blinding of old Gloucester) taking place. He will not stand it. His sword is out and pointed at his master's breast in a moment: then Regan stabs him dead from behind. That is his whole part: eight lines all told. But if it were real life and not a play, that is the part it would be best to have acted.

The doctrine of the Second Coming teaches us that we do not and cannot know when the world drama will end. The curtain may be rung down at any moment: say, before you have finished reading this paragraph. This seems to some people intolerably frustrating. So many things would be interrupted. Perhaps you were going to get married next month, perhaps you were going to get a raise next week: you may be on the verge of a great scientific discovery; you may be maturing great social and political reforms. Surely no good and wise God would be so very unreasonable as to cut all this short? Not *now*, of all moments!

But we think thus because we keep on assuming that we know the play. We do not know the play. We do not even know whether we are in Act I or Act V. We do not know who are the major and who the minor characters. The Author knows. The audience, if there is an audience (if angels and archangels and all the company of heaven fill the pit and the stalls) may have an inkling. But we, never seeing the play from outside, never meeting any characters except the tiny minority who are "on" in the same scenes as ourselves, wholly igno-

rant of the future and very imperfectly informed about
the past, cannot tell at what moment the end ought to
come. That it will come when it ought, we may be sure;
but we waste our time in guessing when that will be.
That it has a meaning we may be sure, but we cannot
see it. When it is over, we may be told. We are led to
expect that the Author will have something to say to
each of us on the part that each of us has played. The
playing it well is what matters infinitely.

The doctrine of the Second Coming, then, is not to
be rejected because it conflicts with our favorite modern mythology. It is, for that very reason, to be the more
valued and made more frequently the subject of medi-
tation. It is the medicine our condition especially needs.

And with that, I turn to the practical. There is a real
difficulty in giving this doctrine the place which it ought
to have in our Christian life without, at the same time,
running a certain risk. The fear of that risk probably
deters many teachers who accept the doctrine from saying very much about it.

We must admit at once that this doctrine has, in the
past, led Christians into very great follies. Apparently
many people find it difficult to believe in this great
event without trying to guess its date, or even without
accepting as a certainty the date that any quack or hys-
teric offers them. To write a history of all these ex-
ploded predictions would need a book, and a sad, sordid,
tragi-comical book it would be. One such prediction was
circulating when St. Paul wrote his second letter to the
Thessalonians. Someone had told them that "the Day"

was "at hand." This was apparently having the result which such predictions usually have: people were idling and playing the busybody. One of the most famous predictions was that of poor William Miller in 1843. Miller (whom I take to have been an honest fanatic) dated the Second Coming to the year, the day, and the very minute. A timely comet fostered the delusion. Thousands waited for the Lord at midnight on March 21st, and went home to a late breakfast on the 22nd followed by the jeers of a drunkard.

Clearly, no one wishes to say anything that will reawaken such mass hysteria. We must never speak to simple, excitable people about "the Day" without emphasizing again and again the utter impossibility of prediction. We must try to show them that that impossibility is an essential part of the doctrine. If you do not believe our Lord's words, why do you believe in his return at all? And if you do believe them must you not put away from you, utterly and forever, any hope of dating that return? His teaching on the subject quite clearly consisted of three propositions. (1) That he will certainly return. (2) That we cannot possibly find out when. (3) And that therefore we must always be ready for him.

Note the *therefore*. Precisely because we cannot predict the moment, we must be ready at all moments. Our Lord repeated this practical conclusion again and again; as if the promise of the Return had been made for the sake of this conclusion alone. Watch, watch, is the burden of his advice. I shall come like a thief. You will not,

I most solemnly assure you you will not, see me approaching. If the householder had known at what time the burglar would arrive, he would have been ready for him. If the servant had known when his absent employer would come home, he would not have been found drunk in the kitchen. But they didn't. Nor will you. Therefore you must be ready at all times. The point is surely simple enough. The schoolboy does not know which part of his Virgil lesson he will be made to translate: that is why he must be prepared to translate *any* passage. The sentry does not know at what time an enemy will attack, or an officer inspect, his post: that is why he must keep awake *all* the time. The Return is wholly unpredictable. There will be wars and rumours of wars and all kinds of catastrophes, as there always are. Things will be, in that sense, normal, the hour before the heavens roll up like a scroll. You cannot guess it. If you could, one chief purpose for which it was foretold would be frustrated. And God's purposes are not so easily frustrated as that. One's ears should be closed against any future William Miller in advance. The folly of listening to him at all is almost equal to the folly of believing him. He *couldn't* know what he pretends, or thinks, he knows.

Of this folly George MacDonald has written well. "Do those," he asks, "who say, Lo here or lo there are the signs of his coming, think to be too keen for him and spy his approach? When he tells them to watch lest he find them neglecting their work, they stare this way and that, and watch lest he should succeed in coming like a thief! Obedience is the one key of life."

The doctrine of the Second Coming has failed, so far as we are concerned, if it does not make us realize that at every moment of every year in our lives Donne's question "What if this present were the world's last night?" is equally relevant.

Sometimes this question has been pressed upon our minds with the purpose of exciting fear. I do not think that is its right use. I am, indeed, far from agreeing with those who think all religious fear barbarous and degrading and demand that it should be banished from the spiritual life. Perfect love, we know, casteth out fear. But so do several other things—ignorance, alcohol, passion, presumption, and stupidity. It is very desirable that we should all advance to that perfection of love in which we shall fear no longer; but it is very undesirable, until we have reached that stage, that we should allow any inferior agent to cast out our fear. The objection to any attempt at perpetual trepidation about the Second Coming is, in my view, quite a different one: namely, that it will certainly not succeed. Fear is an emotion: and it is quite impossible—even physically impossible—to maintain any emotion for very long. A perpetual excitement of hope about the Second Coming is impossible for the same reason. Crisis-feeling of any sort is essentially transitory. Feelings come and go, and when they come a good use can be made of them: they cannot be our regular spiritual diet.

What is important is not that we should always fear (or hope) about the End but that we should always remember, always take it into account. An analogy may here help. A man of seventy need not be always feeling (much less talking) about his approaching death: but a wise man of seventy should always take it into account. He would be foolish to embark on schemes which presuppose twenty more years of life: he would be criminally foolish not to make—indeed, not to have made long since—his will. Now, what death is to each man, the Second Coming is to the whole human race. We all believe, I suppose, that a man should "sit loose" to his own individual life, should remember how short, precarious, temporary, and provisional a thing it is; should never give all his heart to anything which will end when his life ends. What modern Christians find it harder to remember is that the whole life of humanity in this world is also precarious, temporary, provisional.

Any moralist will tell you that the personal triumph of an athlete or of a girl at a ball is transitory: the point is to remember that an empire or a civilisation is also transitory. All achievements and triumphs, in so far as they are merely this-worldly achievements and triumphs, will come to nothing in the end. Most scientists here join hands with the theologians; the earth will not always be habitable. Man, though longer-lived than men, is equally mortal. The difference is that whereas the scientists expect only a slow decay from within, we reckon with sudden interruption from without—at any moment. ("What if this present were the world's last night?")

Taken by themselves, these considerations might seem to invite a relaxation of our efforts for the good of posterity: but if we remember that what may be upon us at any moment is not merely an End but a Judgment, they should have no such result. They may, and should, correct the tendency of some moderns to talk as though duties to posterity were the only duties we had. I can imagine no man who will look with more horror on the End than a conscientious revolutionary who has, in a sense sincerely, been justifying cruelties and injustices inflicted on millions of his contemporaries by the benefits which he hopes to confer on future generations: generations who, as one terrible moment now reveals to him, were never going to exist. Then he will see the massacres, the faked trials, the deportations, to be all ineffaceably real, an essential part, his part, in the drama that has just ended: while the future Utopia had never been anything but a fantasy.

Frantic administration of panaceas to the world is certainly discouraged by the reflection that "this present" might be "the world's last night"; sober work for the future, within the limits of ordinary morality and prudence, is not. For what comes is Judgment: happy are those whom it finds labouring in their vocations, whether they were merely going out to feed the pigs or laying good plans to deliver humanity a hundred years hence from some great evil. The curtain has indeed now fallen. Those pigs will never in fact be fed, the great campaign against White Slavery or Governmental Tyranny will never in fact proceed to victory. No matter; you were at your post when the Inspection came.

Our ancestors had a habit of using the word "Judgment" in this context as if it meant simply "punishment": hence the popular expression, "It's a judgment on him." I believe we can sometimes render the thing more vivid to ourselves by taking judgment in a stricter sense: not as the sentence or award, but as the Verdict. Some day (and "What if this present were the world's last night?") an absolutely correct verdict—if you like, a perfect critique—will be passed on what each of us is.

We have all encountered judgments or verdicts on ourselves in this life. Every now and then we discover what our fellow creatures really think of us. I don't of course mean what they tell us to our faces: that we usually have to discount. I am thinking of what we sometimes overhear by accident or of the opinions about us which our neighbours or employees or subordinates unknowingly reveal in their actions: and of the terrible, or lovely, judgments artlessly betrayed by children or even animals. Such discoveries can be the bitterest or sweetest experiences we have. But of course both the bitter and the sweet are limited by our doubt as to the wisdom of those who judge. We always hope that those who so clearly think us cowards or bullies are ignorant and malicious; we always fear that those who trust us or admire us are misled by partiality. I suppose the experience of the Final Judgment (which may break in upon us at any moment) will be like these little experiences, but magnified to the Nth.

For it will be infallible judgment. If it is favorable we shall have no fear, if unfavorable, no hope, that it is wrong. We shall not only believe, we shall know, know beyond doubt in every fibre of our appalled or delighted being, that as the Judge has said, so we are: neither more nor less nor other. We shall perhaps even realise that in some dim fashion we could have known it all along. We shall know and all creation will know too: our ancestors, our parents, our wives or husbands, our children. The unanswerable and (by then) self-evident truth about each will be known to all.

I do not find that pictures of physical catastrophe—that sign in the clouds, those heavens rolled up like a scroll—help one so much as the naked idea of Judgment. We cannot always be excited. We can, perhaps, train ourselves to ask more and more often how the thing which we are saying or doing (or failing to do) at each moment will look when the irresistible light streams in upon it; that light which is so different from the light of this world—and yet, even now, we know just enough of it to take it into account. Women sometimes have the problem of trying to judge by artificial light how a dress will look by daylight. That is very like the problem of all of us: to dress our souls not for the electric lights of the present world but for the daylight of the next. The good dress is the one that will face that light. For that light will last longer.

Books by C. S. Lewis
available from Harcourt, Inc.
in Harvest paperback editions

All My Road Before Me: The Diary of C. S. Lewis, 1922 –1927
The Business of Heaven: Daily Readings from C. S. Lewis
The Dark Tower and Other Stories
The Four Loves
Letters of C. S. Lewis
Letters to Malcolm: Chiefly on Prayer
A Mind Awake: An Anthology of C. S. Lewis
Narrative Poems
Of Other Worlds: Essays and Stories
On Stories: And Other Essays on Literature
Poems
Present Concerns
Reflections on the Psalms
Spirits in Bondage: A Cycle of Lyrics
Surprised by Joy: The Shape of My Early Life
Till We Have Faces: A Myth Retold
The World's Last Night and Other Essays

Also available in
Harvest paperback editions

C. S. Lewis at the Breakfast Table and Other Reminiscences,
edited by James T. Como

C. S. Lewis: A Biography,
by Roger Lancelyn Green and Walter Hooper

The Literary Legacy of C. S. Lewis,
by Chad Walsh